BLACK MESA
The Angel of Death

BLACK MESA
The Angel of Death

by Suzanne Gordon
With Photographs by
Alan Copeland

The John Day Company
New York

Copyright © 1973 by Suzanne Gordon and
Alan Copeland

Library of Congress Cataloging in Publication Data

Gordon, Suzanne, 1945-
    Black Mesa.

    Bibliography: p.
    1. Electric power-plants—Environmental aspects—
Southwest, New. 2. Strip mining—Environmental
aspects—Black Mesa, Ariz. 3. Hopi Indians—Government
relations. 4. Coal mines and mining—Arizona—Black
Mesa. 5. Black Mesa, Ariz. I. Title.
TD195.E4G67   301.24'3'0979135   72-12082
ISBN 0-381-98239-4
ISBN 0-381-90006-1 (pbk)

The John Day Company, 257 Park Avenue
South, New York, N.Y. 10010

Published on the same day in Canada by Long-
man Canada Limited.

Printed in the United States of America

Book   design by Constance T. Doyle

For
My Mother
and
Judi and Richard

Acknowledgments

I would like to thank members of the Black Mesa Defense Fund for their unending cooperation in making this book possible: Mr. James Hopper, Mr. Terrence Moore, and Mr. Tom Andrews. Mr. Bruce Greene of the Native American Rights Fund provided legal information and advice, and Jonathan Adler of the National Health and Environmental Law Program at the University of California (Los Angeles) also gave me valuable information concerning the legal aspects of the Black Mesa cases.

Dr. John List at the California Institute of Technology has my special thanks for his unending aid and technical advice, as does Mr. Lloyd Linford for editorial assistance and support.

The following people in the electrical utilities industry were kind enough to provide me with interviews and information: Mr. Edward Nelson of Chickering and Gregory, counsel to San Diego Gas and Electric. Mr. Greg Nesbitt and C.M. Lafoon of San Diego Gas and Electric; Mr. David Fogarty of Southern California Edison; Mr. Floyd L. Goss of the Los Angeles Department of Water and Power; and Mr. Jack Swift of the Arizona Public Service Company.

Our appreciation is also extended to Mr. Robert Hilgendorf of the Chinle Branch of DNA, Navajo Legal Services; the Committee of Concern for the Traditional Indian in San Francisco; Mr. Tom Tarbet of the Committee for Traditional Indian Land and Life in Los Angeles; and to Dr. John Goffman of the Livermore Scientific Laboratory for informational assistance.

I would also like to acknowledge Harold Courlander's book *Fourth World of the Hopi* and Frank Water's *Book of the Hopi*, as well as discussions with Thomas and Vermina Banyaca of New Oraibi on the Hopi mesas for information they provided for my introductory chapter on the Hopi legend and prophecy.

But my most special thanks go to my friends who were always present to give me their moral support—Peter Fehler, Pat Tavenner, and Wilma, Stan and Nancy Keller.

TRANSMISSION SYSTEM

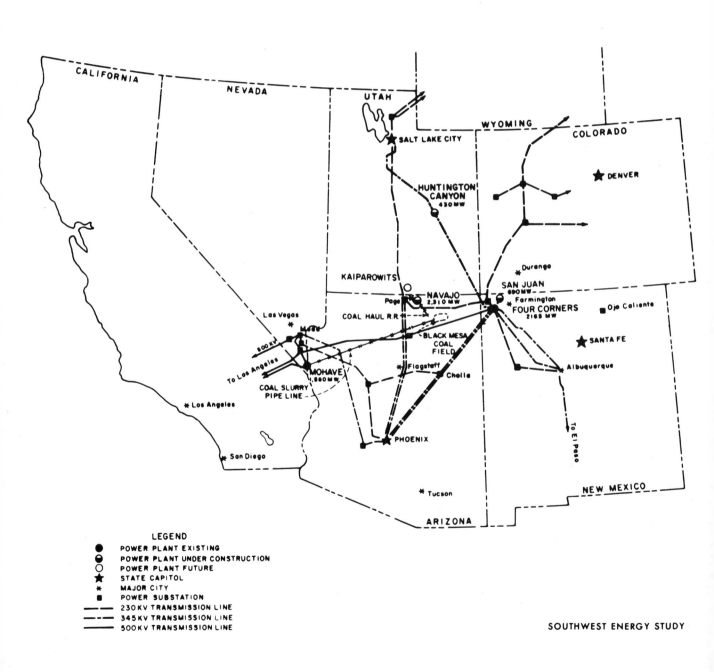

CALIFORNIA

NEVADA

UTAH

WYOMING

COLORADO

SALT LAKE CITY

HUNTINGTON
CANYON
430MW

DENVER

KAIPAROWITS

Durango

SAN JUAN
890MW

Page

NAVAJO
2,310 MW

Farmington
FOUR CORNERS
2165 MW

Ojo Caliente

Las Vegas

COAL HAUL R.R.

Mead

SANTA FE

500 KV

BLACK MESA
COAL FIELD

Albuquerque

To Los Angeles

Flagstaff

Cholla

MOHAVE
860MW

COAL SLURRY
PIPE LINE

To El Paso

Los Angeles

PHOENIX

San Diego

NEW MEXICO

Tucson

ARIZONA

LEGEND

● POWER PLANT EXISTING
◐ POWER PLANT UNDER CONSTRUCTION
○ POWER PLANT FUTURE
★ STATE CAPITOL
✳ MAJOR CITY
■ POWER SUBSTATION
— — — 230 KV TRANSMISSION LINE
— · — 345 KV TRANSMISSION LINE
——— 500 KV TRANSMISSION LINE

SOUTHWEST ENERGY STUDY

COAL RESOURCES

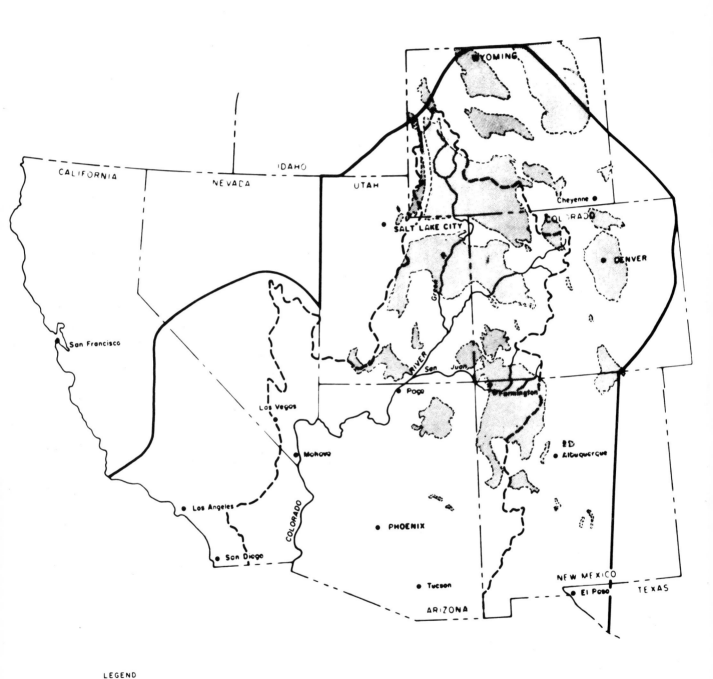

SOUTHWEST ENERGY STUDY

Prepared by
POWER DEVELOPMENT AND ECONOMIC
EFFECTS WORK GROUP

Contents

BLACK
MESA
The
Angel
of
Death

INTRODUCTION ⨳ THE PROPHECY

The Hopi are an old people. Their faces read like maps of the land on which they live, creased and dry like the washes that carry occasional summer rain to the fields, cheekbones set high, like the mesas that have been their home since before the coming of the white man, since before even the Navajo wandered across the desert. The Hopi's history and religion are bound to the land; and the Hopi are its protectors, responding to each movement of the universe with a prayer of celebration or grief. Even their homes are built into the land, stone, no taller than a man, as if they did not wish to climb higher than their mother earth.

The Hopi land lies in the area known as Four Corners, a region famous among geographers and schoolchildren as the intersection of the borders of Utah, Colorado, Arizona, and New Mexico. It is to the Southwest what the Mississippi Delta is to the South. It is arid land, and, to the outsider's eye, hostile. But to the Hopi, it

Adam Clark Vromar, Hopi

is the center of the universe, and the central stage for a drama of cosmic significance.

In Hopi mythology, Four Corners is the center of their fourth world. Their first world was called *Topkela*, endless space. In it, the chosen people, the Hopi and others who were faithful to the way of the Great Spirit, lived in harmony, health and plenty—a harmony that would last only as long as the people obeyed the teachings of the Great Spirit.

Some did not. The Great Spirit ordered the destruction of the first world, telling those who had remembered his ways that he would hide them where they would be safe when fire and water covered *Topkela*.

The chosen people hid from the destruction of the first world and then went to the second, called *Topka*, where there was harmony until it was broken by the presence of evil. The Great Spirit was again forced to protect his way, and those who followed it. He destroyed the second world and

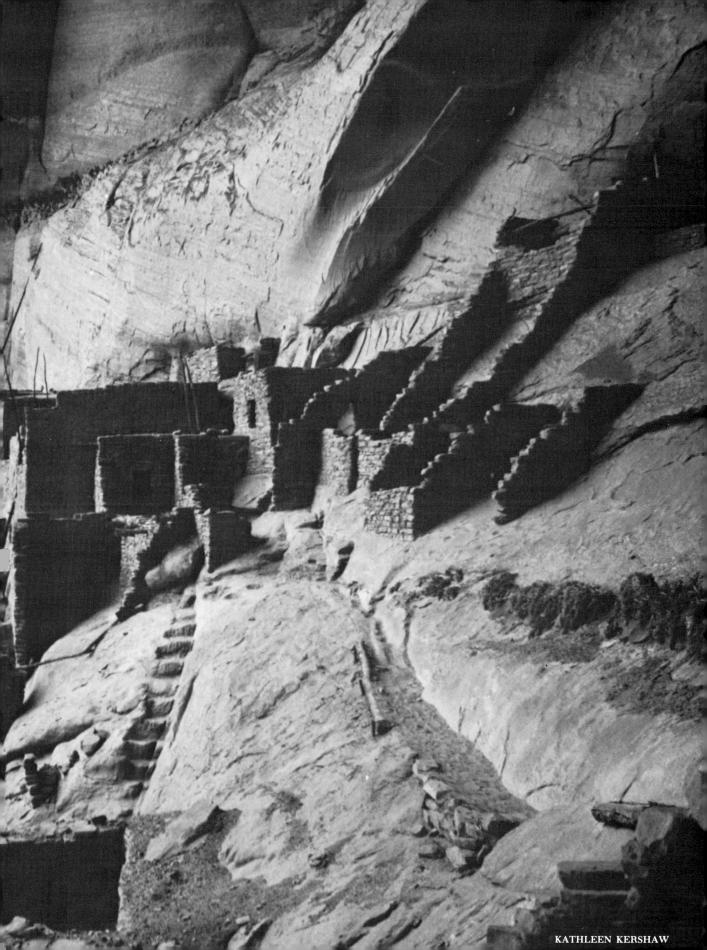

prepared the people for the third. There, in *Kuskurza*, the people lived together in large cities, at peace with nature. But, for the third time, war and sexual license forced the Great Spirit to destroy the world.

After the fall of *Kuskurza*, the chosen people searched for a new world. They sent a messenger to find what lay above the sky and see if it might not be the fourth world. The messenger, the catbird, flew up and up until it found an opening in the sky that led to the fourth world. There it found the Spirit of Death, owner of fire, and master of the fourth world, *Masauwu*. The Spirit of Death said he would let the people come through the skies and live with him in this land.

The people had to find a way through the sky, to the *Sipapuni*, the doorway in the sky. They planted a seed that became a high reed that grew until it reached the *Sipapuni*. The people climbed, the Hopi waiting until last. To this day, Hopi *Kivas*, or places of prayer, are built into the ground, with the only exit being a ladder, in commemoration of the Hopi's emergence through the *Sipapuni* into the fourth world.

When they entered the fourth world, the people were given ears of corn to choose from. The Hopi again waited until last and, showing their humility, chose the poorest ear of blue corn, which promised them much suffering but a long life. The Great Spirit allowed them entrance, instructing them to keep the land in trust until he

Overleaf: Near Black Mesa: homes of the Hopi ancestors

Near Black Mesa

Hopi prayer sanctuary on the Mesa

returned to claim it. They have maintained their stewardship. They still continue to live as they have for centuries, refusing to adopt the "improvements" of modern technology. It is a way of life they have chosen: the caretakers of the land.

There was among the chosen people, the legend says, a white man, the *Bahana,* the lost white brother that runs through the legends of almost all the Indians of the Americas. He left his brothers the Hopi and went toward the land of the rising sun, carrying half a stone tablet that he would keep with him until the day he returned with gifts of harmony and peace for his brothers. The Hopi would know him by matching his half tablet with the half tablet they still have in their possession today. But should the *Bahana* fail to return, the Hopi would be threatened by destruction.

The Hopi were told to wander across the new world, leaving markings and ruins along their way. They were to search for the appointed place, a place they would recognize once they had reached it. It would be their center. Clan by clan the Hopi began their migration. Some failed to complete the journey, but the faithful reached their destination—the three mesas and the high desert country where they live today. As each clan arrived, it sought permission from those who had come before, to settle.

The Hopi have lived on these sacred mesas for more than seven hundred years, which makes their village Oraibi the oldest continuously inhabited settlement in the United States. In this arid desert, where ties between man and god are necessary to sustain life, they have warded off hostile tribes, encroaching Navajos, and Spanish conquistadores. Yet throughout their troubled history, the Hopi have remained faithful to their way of peace, as the prophecy in the legend foretold.

Nevertheless, the prophecy predicts one great threat to come, one last test of faith and endurance. It will arrive, according to the legend, in the form of a new race of people, who will come to the mesas bearing promises of a better life, of "progress" for the Hopi. But the promises, if accepted, will prove false; the strangers will steal the Hopi lands and destroy their culture. And if the promises are not accepted, the strangers will adopt other means of persuasion—weapons of violence, treachery, and division of the tribe—until the Hopi too choose violence and abandon their ways of peace.

The evil will come, the prophecy says, after certain events have taken place, as omens of the days of struggle. Among these signs are natural disasters, earthquakes, floods, famine, and a change in the weather, such that the warm places of the earth turn cold, and the cold places hot. Roads will be built in the sky carrying men where they have never been, and a gourd of ashes will be dropped on the earth, boiling and causing great destruction. In the final stage, people bearing a peculiar sign—the sign of the swastika—will shake the world into war. They

will be defeated the first time but will rise and make war again. Again, defeat will come; yet they will rise a third time.

It is this third war, the Hopi say, which will settle their fate and that of the rest of mankind. If their white brother does not come to save them, the four forces of nature will come from the east, "like ants crawling across the land."

And in the whole world, only Four Corners will be a sanctuary, for it is to this place that all good people will come when the day of purification arrives. If this land too is destroyed, there will be no hope for man, and all life will vanish.

To many observers, Indian and non-Indian alike, the scheme of Hopi mythology is of more than a passing anthropological interest. For the legend contains a series of nearly incredible coincidences with unfolding history, coincidences that run deeper than the identification of a *race* of invaders, or of men marked by swastikas, or of a great world war. To people as far removed from the Hopi tradition as hydrologists and medical doctors, the prophecy of the destruction of the earth is becoming a reality, with consequences nearly as dire as those predicted by the Hopi legend. Now, with the destruction of Black Mesa, the sacred mountain, for coal to fuel enormous power-generating plants nearby, the Hopi elders say the last test has begun.

ONE

⧉

THE
FALSE
BROTHERS

We Hopi knew all this would come about because this is the Universal plan. It was planned
by the Great Spirit and the Creator that when
the white man came he would offer us many
things. If we were to accept those offers from
his government, that would be the doom of the
Hopi nation.
(from *The Planting Stick: Hopi Teachings
and Prophecies from the Beginning of Life
to the Day of Purification* as told by Dan
Katchongva, Sun Clan.)

Black Mesa is barren land with little
water, covered with brush and juniper
and piñon trees. To the Navajo and
Hopi Indians, on whose reservation in
northeastern Arizona the 3,300-
square-mile plateau sits, Black Mesa
has always been part of the miracle of
creation. If life can continue amidst
endless miles of rock and dust, their
gods must be real and present.

The Hopi Indians use the mesa as a
burial ground for their dead, a sacred
center whose destruction presages the
destruction of the earth. The Navajo
call it the Female Mountain, and

Mojave Plant

nearby *Lukachukai* the Male Mountain, symbols of the balance of nature
which it is the Navajo's duty to preserve.

And now Black Mesa has become
the focus of perhaps the greatest ecological crisis of our decade.

Nature, the Indians say, must be
left in peace. But despite their plead-
ings war has come, with huge shovels
that scoop out the earth and robotlike
power lines that stalk across the desert
like creatures from a science fiction
movie waiting only for word from an
unknown planet to act and conquer
the earth.

In 1911, geologists discovered on Black Mesa what is believed to be some of the most extensive deposits of coal known in the world; soft-bituminous, low-sulfur coal, worth millions. The coal is deposited relatively close to the surface of the earth, making it accessible by strip-mining processes. In the 1960's, Peabody Coal Company, a wholly owned subsidiary of Kennecott Copper, began a long series of negotiations to mine Black Mesa coal.

Peabody's coal will be used to fuel two power plants: the Mojave Plant in Bullhead City, Nevada, and the Navajo Plant in Page, Arizona. These two plants are part of a huge power grid composed of six plants being planned and contructed for the Southwest by a power consortium of twenty-three semi-private, state, municipal, and federal companies and agencies together called Western Supply and Transmission Associates—or WEST.

The most notorious plant to date in the WEST grid is located at Four Corners. The Four Corners Plant alone daily produces 2,075 megawatts of electrical power and more emissions of sulfur and nitrogen oxides than are released in Los Angeles and New York City combined, plus huge quantities of particulate filth, and no one knows how much mercury and radioactive trace elements. American astronauts circling the earth found the plume of pollution from Four Corners to be the only evidence of man's presence in the Southwest.

The six plants in the WEST grid will supply electrical power to Southern California, the Tucson-Phoenix area, central Arizona, Las Vegas, and areas in New Mexico, Utah, and Colorado. They will also supply enough pollutants to make of the Southwest a smog basin extending from the Rocky Mountains to Southern California—blackening the skies over six National Parks, three National Recreation Areas, twenty-eight National Monuments, and countless state parks and historic landmarks.

The mining of Black Mesa and the construction of the WEST plants will do more than take coal from the land and pollute the air. It will draw from the desert one of its most precious commodities—water. Peabody's coal must travel a considerable distance to reach the power plants it fuels. The Navajo Plant, some eighty miles from Black Mesa, is serviced by a coal train. But the Mojave Plant is 275 miles away; and Peabody found it would be cheaper to send the coal that distance in a slurry pipeline, in which the coal is crushed to a fine dust and then mixed with water. The cost to the environment and people of the Southwest is 2,700 gallons of water per minute, which must be pumped from far beneath the surface of the desert.

This water (along with thousands of acre-feet per year drawn from the Colorado River and used for cooling the plants) will be fed to machines that will soil it with chemicals and silt. It will then be returned to the land, air, and rivers, still heavily polluted, to be

Four Corners plant

absorbed by the harvests of the thirty-nine Indian tribes living in the area, and the agricultural valleys of California and Mexico.

The land of the Southwest will be ripped apart, the water and air polluted, to deliver power to Los Angeles and Southern California because that area has been so overpolluted that no more generating plants may be constructed in the Los Angeles Basin. In fact, the WEST plants would exceed Los Angeles pollution standards by between 100 and 1,000 times. But the demand for power is constantly increasing, and the utilities companies insist they need more plants to meet the "needs" of the people.

The Southwest, remote and sparsely populated, seems the perfect site for the plants. There are supplies of cheap coal nearby, water from the Colorado and San Juan rivers, and the sharp, clean air of the desert. In so pure an environment presumably, a great deal of pollution could be generated before anyone would notice.

Politically, too, the Four Corners area was ideal. For more than twenty years, Arizona had been struggling to put its share of Colorado River water to use and had been prevented from doing so by California and, among others, Utah. With the promise of cheap electric power to fuel the water pumps and buy the goodwill of its neighbors, Arizona could at last implement the great irrigation project—the Central Arizona Project (CAP).

This game plan, apparently agreed to in the early sixties by the State of Arizona, a consortium of public utilities, and the United States Government, failed to comprehend one factor —the Hopi and Navajos who not only cared deeply about the land, but who actually owned much of it. Without even consulting the tribes, the Department of the Interior, functioning as the Indians' legal guardian, approved the leasing arrangements of

Hopi and Navajo land to Peabody Coal. Subsequently, and on the advice of Interior agents, the Hopi and Navajo Tribal Councils approved leasing contracts. Signed by the Navajo Council in 1964 and the Hopi Council two years later, the agreements granted Peabody the right to mine Black Mesa for thirty-five years.

Although fought with different weapons, the strategy of Interior and the coal and utilities companies constitutes a very old-fashioned Indian war. Today the techniques have simply changed, as the Hopi prophecy predicted. Artillery and horse soldiers have been replaced by turbines and generators. The genocide will thus be

less direct. Instead of pumping lead into Indian bellies, the attackers will pump ash into the air, saline into the rivers, and pull precious water from the land. The Indians will die because the land will die; the balance upon which they depend will break, and the tribes will be broken with it.

But these new weapons will affect not only Indians and their culture. This last attack on the Indians promises to be truly democratic. The clouds of ash and gas, the salt and chemicals replacing the water of our rivers, will join with pollutants from other factories of death in this country that in the name of profit bring us only a quicker end. When the Southwest has been mined and pummeled and drilled, all to bring the ordinary citizens what industry so diligently convinces him he needs, there will be no place left to go.

The air that poisons the Indians' life and land, unlike the Angel of Death visiting revenge upon Pharaoh, cannot tell white from Indian, rich from poor, and has no eyes with which to view the markings of the Chosen people. Pollution will not pass over, it will pass on—to all of us.

TWO
⋶⋶
THE
BIG ROCK
CANDY MOUNTAIN

In the Big Rock Candy Mountain
There's a land that's fair and bright
Where the handouts grow on bushes
And you sleep out every night.
(American folksong)

WEST promises that progress will be the result of its efforts to electrify the landscape of the Southwest. Progress may come from the rape of the land, but few of its fruits will go to the Indians. They will get only the ash and the acid.

It's an old and familiar story, one that begins, as far as Black Mesa is concerned, with the passage of the Indian Reorganization Act in 1935. The Act replaced the Indians' indigenous form of government, the village chiefs, with Tribal Councils—a supposedly democratically elected representative governing body. Under the guise of making the reservations safe for democracy, the Tribal Councils have

Tuba City, Arizona

merely provided the federal government and the developers with "puppet" governments, easily accessible bodies that will act speedily to grant decisions favorable to industry. Had the village chief system of government remained intact, such decisions would have required the consent of each village chief, a difficult if not impossible thing to obtain.

From the beginning of this white man's game, Hopi leaders and a great majority of the tribe have boycotted the Tribal Council, which has brought not democracy, but rather great divisions in the tribe between "Progressives," who favor the white man's ways, and the "Traditionals," who prefer the old ways.

Thomas Bunyaca, Hopi

In 1935, only 671 out of 4,000 Hopi voted to establish the Council, and continued opposition to the Council has often gone as far as open sabotage of its decisions. Recently, Traditionals have taken the extraordinary step of suing WEST and the Department of the Interior in an attempt to halt the plants. Traditional Hopi have never before resorted to the white man's courts to settle tribal disputes. They have consistently asserted that the land is theirs and no one, especially the U.S. Government, has any right to decide how it should be used.

The Traditionalist view of the white man's courts and legal system may be made clear by an examination of the man who represents the Hopi Tribal Council. John S. Boyden of Salt Lake City is a bishop of the Mormon Church, a religion that holds that Indians, if they are very, very good, may be reincarnated as whites. Boydon has been representing the Hopi Tribal Council since 1951. The Council and a number of other Indian tribes have become the mainstay of his legal practice, a practice which has brought him great monetary profit. His representation of the Indians has been accompanied by numerous complaints of unethical conduct. One of his clients, the Aneth Extension Navajo, for instance, recently brought suit against him for alleged misadministration of an oil royalties fund. And according to Hopi Traditional leader John Lansa, Traditionals accuse Boyden of conflict of interest when he negotiated oil and gas exploration rights on their land. Lansa and others claim Boyden was representing both the oil and gas companies and the Tribal Council during that deal. Boyden has zealously pushed for mineral leases between the Hopi and industry. This zeal may be explained by the large sums of money he gains as a result of such negotiations.

SUZANNE GORDON

Traditionals have further alleged that Boyden was guilty of misconduct in his negotiations concerning the Black Mesa Mine. They say Boyden failed to inform the Council of its legal rights, its real bargaining power, and of the potential environmental effects of the mine.

Perhaps the most serious question stemming from Boyden's connection with the Hopi is the lack of concern it

the companies and the Indian tribes. A vice-president of Southern California Edison, David Fogarty, for example, said in a recent interview that the Hopi who are against the plant are only dissidents spurred on by outside agitators. "I think that one thing that could be happening is that some dissident people in the Indian tribe are against the plants and mine," he insisted. "I don't know what percentage of

has generated in the Department of Interior, which must approve all legal representatives of Indian tribes. Interior has consistently backed Boyden's actions and has never investigated Hopi complaints against him. At the very least, one must assume that Interior's silence implies approval of his less than thorough performance.

Representatives of WEST and Peabody Coal swear by the legality of the contracts Boyden negotiated between

the tribe this is, but in any organized society there is always one sector that's unhappy with the leadership, elected or appointed, or however they got there. I think that those people are being used by people who want to show the power project in the worst light."

And when a friend of the Hopi Traditionals asked the vice-president in charge of public relations of Peabody Coal, William L. Stockton, why his

company so blatantly ignored the true representatives of the Hopi in favor of the Tribal Council, Stockton commented that it would be too difficult for Peabody to go to every village chief and get his permission to lease the land. Peabody needed a quick, easy way of securing leases, and the Tribal Council, created by the Department of the Interior, was a convenient solution.

The participation of the Department of the Interior, the agency designated to protect all our land, in the rape of Black Mesa and the Southwest extends much further than the mere creation of the Tribal Council and the approval of its lawyer. With changes in rhetoric along the way, Interior has been involved for years in industry's attempt to gain control of Indian land, so newly found wealth could be exploited. The Hopi and Navajo, far from being the wards of Interior, are its victims.

In 1948, Interior's Bureau of Indian Affairs called its policies "relocation," or getting the Indian off the reservation and into cities, where he would no longer be the financial responsibility of the Department and his lands would be freed for industrial use.

In 1953, it was "termination," a policy which promised to grant Indians full citizenship, but whose real effect was to deny Indians federal funds and the few privileges that they had and to open Indian lands to developers. The policy eventually resulted in the abolition of several Indian tribes.

And in 1966, the policy emerged as the Indian Resources and Development Act, which the Department told businessmen had two purposes: "(1) the creation of employment opportunities for American Indians and *(2) development of opportunities and profits for your businesses*" (our emphasis).

By 1967, it was no longer fashionable to talk of either termination or exploiting the reservations, and the Indian Resources Act died in committee. Instead, Interior spoke of giving Indians "ultimate independence." In practice, this "independence" means assimilation and cultural genocide, and an entrance to white culture at an appropriate level—the bottom, thus allowing maximum benefit for those at the top.

Even Secretary of the Interior Stewart Udall, of the Johnson administration, generally an enlightened politician, subscribed to this view. "When one looks at Indian resources," he commented, "one asks himself the question, 'What would IBM, or AT&T, or Standard Oil of New Jersey do if they owned this particular piece of land and these resources?'"

Udall praised the signing of the leases between Peabody and the Navajos in 1965, promising they would provide "new jobs, large tax benefits, tremendous economic advantages not only in royalties and jobs for two Indian tribes but also for the entire Southwest." He congratulated "all

parties involved in this agreement for taking part in a giant step forward in the development of a formula for joint public and private resource development in the Colorado Basin that will become a model for the Nation." Udall neglected to mention that the receipts by the companies and state and federal agencies far exceeded the monetary gain to either tribe, with Kennecott Copper getting $750,000,000, the Hopi $14,000,000, and the Navajo $58,000,000, money that would be held in trust by Interior until that great day when the tribes were ready for "ultimate independence."

Udall's backslapping came at a time when little attention was focused on Black Mesa and its ecological consequences. By 1971, however, things had changed. When reporters asked Udall why he had so unquestioningly approved the project, he answered much less glowingly: "Everyone does what he thinks is right at the time," adding that he would have "second thoughts" about the project today, and that there would be "more concern for pollution." Asked about the effects of strip mining on the area, he said, "Sure, they make a mess out of it. But it's a semi-arid area, a desert out there." Hardly a fitting sentiment for the protector of our environment, and hardly a comforting concept for the Hopi and Navajo, dwellers on that "desert."

Despite Udall's "second thoughts," Rogers C. B. Morton, head of Interior under the Nixon administration, has refused to reconsider Interior's stand on WEST. It was only on May 7, 1971, after a letter from lawyers representing the Traditional Hopi and Navajo, that Morton announced that Interior would initiate a cumulative study, the *Southwest Energy Study,* of the impact of the six power plants on the environment of the Southwest. Morton was asked to declare a moratorium on construction or permits for five of the plants, pending completion of the study. He denied that request, and instead imposed a moratorium on the Kaiparowitz Plant, an uncontroversial move since the plant is only in the planning stages and there is little to halt.

Construction workers trailer court. Page, Arizona

In March, 1972, the Environmental Protection Agency (EPA) completed its portion of the *Southwest Energy Study* and submitted it to Interior. A press release by the EPA on its findings was mysteriously killed, some believe through pressure from Interior. The EPA findings that were made public, in April, 1972, explained Interior's heated reaction. The study said that, without much stricter pollution control equipment than is now planned for the plants, the Southwest's environment will be "increasingly and significantly degraded by projected power plants in the four

*Indians protesting at Gallup Indian
Festival, New Mexico*

state area," ruining the air and presenting a serious health hazard.

Yet Interior continues to back the plants, and advocates the building of even more plants in the area.

This continued support is perhaps best explained by a series of conflicts of interest that suggest the Department is motivated by political and economic, not environmental or humanistic concerns.

Within the Interior Department are several bureaus, each supposedly with its own areas of responsibility and expertise, and each with its own constituency. In fact, responsibilities overlap and conflicts of interest result.

When this occurs, the conflicts are resolved politically, with the more powerful agencies in the Department getting their way. At Black Mesa, the Secretary of the Interior was bound to consider the wishes of three agencies, two of them—the Bureau of Reclamation and the Bureau of Land Management—very powerful; and one of them—the Bureau of Indian Affairs—very weak.

The Bureau of Reclamation and the Bureau of Land Management have enormous resources, in the form of federally owned land and water and jurisdiction over "public works," which may be allocated at subsidized rates to preferred industries. For many years, both these agencies have

Hopi village on the Mesa

promoted the Central Arizona Project, an irrigation project that has drawn scathing criticism from environmentalists. Interior's support of the CAP at one time included a plan to dam the Colorado River near the Grand Canyon, thus drowning the Canyon under an artificial lake. The goal of the dam was to provide enough electrical power to drive the CAP's water pumps.

When Congress quashed the Grand Canyon plan, Interior switched to backing the Black Mesa mine and WEST plants. The Bureau of Reclamation was given valuable patronage, and 24.3 percent of the total output of the Navajo Plant was to go to the CAP. With so much to gain, it is, perhaps,

small wonder that Interior sided once again with industry over the Indians.

As a partial check on this kind of bias, Congress created, in 1969, the National Environmental Policy Act. The Act stipulates that any federal action that could affect the human environment (such as granting enabling rights for transmission lines, water access roads, etc.) be taken only after the submission of a "detailed statement by the responsible official on (1) the environmental impact of the proposed action, (2) any adverse environmental effects which cannot be avoided should the proposal be implemented, (3) alternatives to the proposed action, (4) the relationship between local short-term uses of man's environment and the maintenance and enhance-

ment of the long-term productivity and (5) any irreversible commitments of resources which would be involved in the proposed action should it be implemented."

Where the WEST plants and mines servicing them are concerned, the Department of the Interior has continued to grant permits *despite* the fact that such environmental impact statements have not been completed.

Such action on the part of Interior reduces the National Environmental Policy Act to the status of a meaningless warning that can have no effect on projects already in progress. But then one wonders what possible effect an Environmental Policy Act could have if its administrators are also owners of the very plants they are judging.

The coal at Black Mesa gleams with a promise of profits and progress. But industry has been guaranteed all the handouts. When the utilities in WEST, the coal companies, and the federal government finish with the Southwest, the Indians will have traded their corn harvests and sheep herds, even their gods, for pollution and Black Lung disease. For the utilities and coal companies Black Mesa is the Big Rock Candy Mountain. But for the rest of us, it is a sample of what industry has in store for us—a world in which its policies of unrestrained growth can only result in unrestrained destruction.

THREE

FIRE

I do not fully understand how the Anglo political system and its laws operate. I cannot comprehend a process which allows people hundreds of miles away to use the resources of other people in a destructive manner. . . . Do people really need electric shoe buffers, toothbrushes, garage door openers, can openers, and hundreds of other modern conveniences? Do people really prefer living in pollution?
(Peterson Zah, Deputy Director
Navajo Legal Agency)

The electrical utilities industry behaves like a cell gone wild—a tumor whose needs have superseded those of its host. Electrical power production is one of the largest industries in the United States, and its managers intend to keep it that way. Industry spokesmen boast of a growth rate in power use of 8 percent per year, with a doubling time of a decade. That the utilities' growth rate threatens to use up most of man's reserves of natural gas, coal, and oil seems, to the industry, irrelevant. That it means releasing ash and oxides of sulfur and nitrogen into the air in staggering quantities is conceded to be a problem, but one

Four Corners plant

which they say has been blown out of all proportion by hysterical environmentalists. That the growth rate, unchecked, will mean a nation overrun with power plants and transmission lines and a nuclear reactor every six miles along its coasts may regrettably be true. But so what? Man must progress. And quality of life will just have to suffer, as that is the price we are forced to pay for electricity.

To satisfy the craving for electricity, the utilities in WEST are building the six coal-fired plants in the Four Corners Region. Almost half of the output of the plants will go to Southern California via the Southern California Edison Company (SCE). SCE is

The Mojave plant

the third largest utility in the country, and its directorate interlocks with some of the West's largest banks and insurance companies. Four of SCE's directors sit on the board of the Pacific Mutual Life Insurance Corporation, the largest insurance company in California, whose president, Asa V. Call, is a very close friend of President Richard M. Nixon, and a trustee of the Nixon Foundation. Other directors serve on the boards of Westernbankcorp., the largest bank holding corporation in the world, and the United California Bank, whose former chairman was Maurice Stans, a man who figured prominently in the recent Watergate Affair. SCE owns 48 percent of

units four and five at Four Corners, 56 percent of the output of the Mojave Plant, and much of the power from the Kaiparowitz plant, planned for Nipple Bench, Utah, on the Kaiparowitz plateau.

At present, only two of the six WEST plants are in operation. Four Corners, a 2,075-megawatt plant, in operation since 1963, is one of the largest coal-fired plants in the world. It is located near Farmington, New Mexico, and is operated by the Arizona Public Service Company (APS), with power consumed by APS, SCE, the Public Service Company of New Mexico, the Salt River Project of Arizona, Tucson Gas and Electric (TG&E), and El Paso Electric. About ten miles northeast of Four Corners is the San Juan Plant, a 990-MW facility, operated by TG&E, with power owned by TG&E and the Public Service Company of New Mexico, which will begin operation in 1973.

The other plant in operation lies some 373 miles southwest of Four Corners, in Bullhead City, Nevada. This is the Mojave Plant, spewing its plume of pollution over the reds and pastels of the Mojave desert. The plant is a 1,580-MW structure, with its power owned by SCE, the Los Angeles Department of Water and Power, the Nevada Power Company, and the Salt River Project.

The other plants in the grid are

Four Corners plant

either in the planning stages or under construction. The 2,310-MW Navajo Plant, in Page, Arizona, on the shores of Lake Powell will be completed in 1976. Twenty-four percent of its power will be bought by the Department of the Interior's Bureau of Reclamation for the Central Arizona Project. Until the Bureau is ready for it, SCE will consume that power, with APS, Nevada Power Company, the Los Angeles Department of Water and Power, and TG&E using the remainder. Some power will also be consumed by the Navajo Tribal Utility Authority, to whom the owners of the plant have benevolently offered electricity at wholesale prices.

Across the shore from Lake Powell

C.M. Laffoon, Vice President,
San Diego Gas & Electric Co.

is the future site of the colossus of the WEST grid—the 5,000- to 6,000-MW Kaiparowitz Plant, which will be the largest coal-fired facility in the world. It is owned by SCE, San Diego Gas and Electric (SDG&E), and the Bureau of Reclamation and will be completed in the early 1980's, perhaps as early as 1984. The Huntington Canyon Plant, in Price, Utah, will complete the WEST grid. This 2,000-MW plant is owned and operated by Utah Power and Light and will be completed in 1974.

These plants will provide 15,000 MW of power upon completion for urban areas in the Southwest. Yet, ac-

cording to present growth estimates, by the 1980's Los Angeles alone will need over 30,000 MW of power. With increased demand in Nevada, Utah, Arizona, and New Mexico, more generating capacity will be needed—presumably to come from plants about which no one has yet told the public. No one, that is, within the electrical utilities industry.

Testimony taken in a series of Congressional hearings concerning electrical power production in the Southwest, held in five cities in 1971, revealed that at least twelve plants have been suggested for Utah, some for Colorado, and some for Southern Nevada. And at a meeting of the Los Angeles Chamber of Commerce on October 16, 1972, Assistant Secretary of the Interior Frank E. Clark, accompanied by representatives of Peabody Coal Company, announced that the Department was recommending the construction of 33,000 megawatts of additional generating plants in the Southwest, 33,000 megawatts over and above the 15,000 represented by the six WEST plants. This makes the "hysterical" projection of a power plant every twenty miles by the year 2030 begin to look like a conservative estimate

The demand for electricity has increased so steeply mainly because electricity is cheap, indiscriminately used, and commercially promoted. In the town of Socorro, New Mexico, for instance, there is one electrical advertising sign for every seven people—

and the town has a population of 5,000.

The industry promotes the use of electricity for all night signs by offering discounts to large consumers of electrical power. This means that large industrial users are encouraged to use more electricity because the more electricity is consumed, the more the consumers' rates decrease. This method of determining price also encourages the expansion of energy-intensive* industries, such as the aluminum industry. It assures that the poor have a much harder time paying their electrical bills than the rich—the cost of electricity is higher for small users. This unequal rate scale may not be a burden on wealthy Americans, but it does mean that the poor will use a larger percentage of their paychecks to pay for electricity than the rich or the heavily polluting industries. But the utilities industry continues to maintain its unequal rates scales, just as it continues to subsidize multimillion-dollar advertising budgets, part of which are spent on anti-environmentalist propaganda.

In 1968, the utilities industry spent, as a whole, $273 million on advertising, compared to $39 million on research and development. In 1969, all utilities spent $320 million on advertising and $41 million on research

* The term "energy-intensive" refers to those modern industries which require enormous use of electrical energy, such as synthetic fibers, aluminum, synthetic rubber, and plastics, all of which use more energy than the alternative product, such as steel or rubber.

and development, an increase of about a third in advertising, and an increase of about two percent on R and D.

And utility advertising seems to serve mainly as a back-up for the appliance industry's campaigns, both in advertising and product development. We now have the indispensable electric toothbrush, electric can opener, electric scissors, electric garage door opener, electric bacon cooker, electric hair curler, electric outdoor grill to make the outdoors like indoors and the electric firelog to make the indoors like outdoors. These appliances do little for the owner except help him spend money. The

John Lansa, Hopi

combination of the proliferation of small appliances and advertising, however, does assure the eight percent growth rate that utilities say is mainly a response to the demand placed upon them by the public.

The increase in electrical energy consumption in the United States may be due to such demands and to the technological advancement of our so-

rate of electrical use is very largely due to expanding energy use by present users and the growth of energy intensive industries—all helped by a friendly shove from your "public" utility.

Facts brought out in the case of the Los Angeles Department of Water and Power vs. the Hearing Board of the Air Pollution Control District of

Las Vegas, Nevada

ciety, but only partially. In the United States, we consume about a third of all the energy used in the world. Other equally technically oriented societies use much less electrical energy. According to the United Nations Statistical Yearbook of 1969, Switzerland, for instance, used 4,026 kilowatt-hours electric per capita and Japan 2,377 KWHE, while the United States used 6,612 KWHE. The continuous growth

the County of Los Angeles in July 1970 revealed that in Los Angeles population increased by 1.75 percent while energy consumption by current consumers increased by 5.8 percent. A look at the *Statistical Report* of the Los Angeles Department of Water and Power helps explain why that increase occurred. The *Report* lauded the fact that 49 percent of the city's new housing units—or 19,475 new dwellings—were "Medallion All

Electric Homes," a concept promoted by the utilities, and that a 485,000-square-foot all-electric convention center had been built, with plans for more all-electric buildings.

The Department claims to be interested in preserving our environment and also bemoans the shortage of natural gas. Yet, an all-electric home actually requires that two to three times as much natural gas be burned to drive generators at the power plant to provide it with the power to run, as a home heated with gas burned directly. But the Department of Water and Power, which uses natural gas to generate fifty percent of its electricity, pushes all-electric, paving the way for the rapid depletion of natural gas, one of the more environmentally sound fuels. Such an attitude is more than irresponsible. The utilities seem to be engaged in a contest to see who can finish off natural gas first.

Because of the growing energy crisis, utilities have faced severe criticism for their advertising policies. The more adaptable members of the industry have halted certain forms of advertising. Southern California Edison and San Diego Gas and Electric no longer advertise openly to increase sales. SCE explained in its yearly statement that it has redirected its advertising revenues to fund promotion of better energy use. Part of that redirection goes to newspaper ads telling people how to curtail or limit electrical use to avoid a possible power shortage in summer months. SCE never tells its customers, however, to buy fewer appliances or to stick to gas heat.

The environmental issue has become the nightmare of the utilities industry. Because of increased awareness by the public the behind-closed-doors dealings that created the six WEST plants are becoming more difficult to carry off. The public is demanding more control over where a power plant is located, the kind of fuel it burns, and what abatement control equipment is installed. This is costing the utilities money and time, and they don't like it. In response, companies like SCE spend thousands of dollars on television ads that proclaim the need to fight overcautious environmentalists who advocate halting power plant construction.

The ads insist that plants must be built to protect the environment. Power, they say, will be needed to clean up the pollution that power plants helped create—or seen another way, environmentally disastrous power plants add to pollution, which we need to clean up, so we need more power plants which will create more pollution, requiring more plants for more clean up, putting out more pollution, and so forth, ad nauseam, smog and increased death rates.

Most utilities, like SCE, advertise to their heart's content because the consumer pays directly for the ads. By law, utilities are guaranteed a six to seven percent annual profit rate, although some make ten and even twenty percent. Advertising expenses are written off as costs and added to the consumers' bill, and the guaranteed profit is thus left intact.

Aside from advertising in local publications, utilities, especially those that may be sensitive to criticism for local ads, channel money to industry associations that take out expensive ads in national publications. The International Electrical Association has sponsored Christmas ads urging people to use more outdoor lighting displays. The Public Service Company of New Mexico and others have begun a television campaign to sell people the idea of "total personal environments" in the home. These environments are of course all electric. These ads are perhaps a subtle way of preparing people for the time when their lives will consist of going from their air-conditioned homes, to their air-conditioned cars, to their air-conditioned offices, and back, without ever breathing the air outside. For if many consumers buy the all-electric concept, the air will be so contaminated by industry's pollutants, helped along by Detroit, that breathing may become a terminal disease.

No one knows better than utility ad men that industrialization and urbanization are great ways to increase sales. The Southwest is gaining population quickly, to the delight of the utilities and the state governments, who gain in additional tax and sales revenues. An example of industry and the government's attitude toward population growth, and their philosophy of land,

resources, and people use, fill the pages of a study done for the Four Corners Regional Development Commission (made up of representatives of Arizona, New Mexico, Utah, and Colorado, plus a federal representative) by the Westinghouse Corporation, concerning the possible development of a new town for the region.

One of the main assets of the new town, of about 100,000 people, would be the industry it could attract. The study claims that an urban center could exist alongside the Indians and Chicanos in the area, "retaining existing cultural and aesthetic values," and that it would furthermore benefit tribes in terms of lease or sale payments for land. But when one reads past the first glittering objectives, one finds that the benefits to industries like the utilities far outweigh any benefit to Indians or the public at large. The interest in the area lies mainly in the fact that land is cheap and that industry can make use of cheap, nonunionized labor and tax breaks.

No clearly defined nucleus is necessary for the growth of manufacturing in the area. Indeed a lack of previous industrial development may actually contain certain benefits. The layouts of older industrial areas, the air and water pollution caused by surrounding industry, the heritage of earlier labor-management conflicts—all these can be avoided by locating in the Four Corners area. *The first to start up in an area gets first claim on a labor supply eager for industrial jobs. Wage levels in rural surroundings are nearly always less than in urban areas. . . .*

Basic to attracting a complex of industries is the idea that there must be a "package" of inducements offered by certain communities in the Four Corners Region. The elements of the "package" are known: an abundant, largely unskilled labor force of undeveloped groups, fine facilities and programs for training labor to specifications of management at *public cost* (such as the ones sponsored by the Bureau of Indian Affairs), prevailing wage rates below those in more specialized sectors of the country, and other industrial development factors combined with the predominantly rural, isolated setting of the Four Corners.

(our emphasis)

Las Vegas, Nevada

Paradise, Nevada

The report to the Commission reflects the utilities' philosophy and uncovers the truth behind the double-talk that what benefits industry benefits all Americans. Peabody Coal, for instance, boasts of a generous grant of $25,000 a year donated to the Navajo Community College. The grant, however, was not made out of the company's largess, on a no-strings basis. Rather, the $25,000 goes to training Indians in technical skills so they will be able to operate machines for the company, which will in turn facilitate the gain that Kennecott makes off the deal.

The utilities claim that cheap electricity is one of America's great strengths, that it provides the motive power for the highest standard of living in the world, a claim that no one disputes. But when industry spokes-men maintain that to limit electrical production at current levels would signal a return to the "good old days" and reduce America to the level of under-developed countries, they are simply promoting tomorrow's profits.

In his testimony at a Congressional Hearing in Las Vegas in 1971, Howard P. Allen, a vice-president of SCE, presented the view that has been repeated over and over again by the utilities:

Staggering quantities of power will be needed for many, many things in the environmental and in the standard-of-living area.

I do not believe that most Americans wish to return to a *primitive* way of life in the hope of achieving an absolute pristine environment. . . .

(our emphasis)

Such statements are examples of the excuses for pollution that the utilities are giving as part of their new "environmental package."

If we curtailed growth in electrical energy consumption today, and kept use at its current level, would Mr. Allen then say that we would be living in a primitive society? Even if we cut back energy consumption to its 1940 level, when we used one-eighth of the electricity we are using today, would that signal a return to a "primitive society"? Hardly, as America enjoyed a very high standard of living in 1940 and had enough power to win a world war fought on two fronts.* But, then,

no one is suggesting reducing energy consumption to the 1940 level anyway.

When utilities executives are not attacking environmentalists on the standard-of-living question, they use another method, concern for the poor, which they have recently developed thanks to the environmental movement. They argue that freezing power consumption at present levels would be to control supply in a context of increasing demand. Caught in a bind between stable supply and rising prices, power would soon be beyond the means of the poor.

This is not an issue in itself, but an

* Although population has increased since 1940, neither that increase, nor the increase of affluence in America is sufficient to explain the astounding growth of electrical energy consumption. According to the Statistical Abstract of the United States, from the years 1946 to 1968 per capita consumption of electrical energy rose 436 percent, while for the same years population increased only 43 percent, and the per capita increase in the Gross National Product was only 59 percent.

obfuscation of the real issue, one that provides the key to the electric power game—rising consumption.

The poor certainly do need electricity, and at reasonable rates, but cheap electricity is hardly the number one demand from America's ghettos and barrios. Full employment and fair wages are, and the utilities' record on employment of blacks and other minority groups, plus their rate scale, clearly tipped in favor of industry and the rich, shows that their real stand on this issue is anything *but* liberal.

Similarly, if the power companies are so concerned about conservation of resources in the poverty sector, why not mobilize some of those highly paid utility lobbyists behind better housing initiatives, to limit the exorbitant

amounts of energy that leak through the holes and cracks of poorly insulated housing and go up the stacks of old and inefficient heating plants in slum buildings?

Finally and most importantly, why not restructure the electric rates themselves, to bring them into line with the realities of power consumption? Everyone, including the contradictory promotional ads of the utilities, concedes that at some point we will reach peak production and will have to limit consumption. So if, as the utilities say, most electricity is consumed by large users, why are the rates adjusted so that these large consumers actually pay far *less* for their power than the poor?

Four Corners plant

The utilities also object to raising their prices to pay for pollution abatement. And again, when a company like SDG&E is asked to spend a bit more on abatement equipment, the poor are paraded out of the file drawer.

"I don't think anyone would argue that pollution shouldn't be controlled to some degree," Greg Nesbitt, an engineer with SDG&E, recently said. "The real question is to what extent? Do you spend $50 million to decrease emissions from a single power plant by one percent? Is that a good way to use people's money? I suspect that if you would ask someone, say in San Diego's lower socio-economic situation, whether he thought that was a good way to spend money, he'd probably say no."

It is interesting that when pollution control is mentioned, suddenly SDG&E begins to talk about consulting the poor. One wonders, however, what the company would say if it were asked to consult the poor on the question of spending money for advertising or executive salaries? What would the poor say when they learned that advertising and sales in 1970 accounted for 0.92 percent of SDG&E's budget and research and development got only 0.406 percent; or for that same year that SCE devoted 1.53 percent of its annual expenditures to advertising and only 0.499 percent to R and D? Would the poor think that was a good use of money?

Furthermore, Nesbitt's comments reveal how the use of percentages can hide the truth. Spending $50 million to decrease emissions even by one percent—which no one has done, by the way—would constitute a significant contribution to pollution abatement. That one percent represents *ten tons* of particulates per day at a plant like Mojave. And that is a lot of ash.

Another tactic the utilities employ to fight environmental criticism is an attempt to make environmentalists look bad, to convince people that although those concerned with the environment claim to be acting in the public interest, they are in fact harming the public, even if this is not deliberate.

In April of 1972, William P. Reilly, president of Arizona Public Service, spoke to a Phoenix television audience and explained that APS's attempt to clean up pollution at Four Corners had resulted in constant malfunctioning at the plant and frequent shutdowns of the entire operation. The problems occurred because APS did not install the most advanced abatement equipment on the plant and had to retrofit equipment whose design and efficiency were unreliable.

"The problems facing us [APS] today," Reilly said, "would not have come about if we had been permitted to install this pollution control equipment in a reasoned and prudent manner. We faced the deadline of December 31, 1971, for completion of all three wet scrubbers [for particulate removal]. We made the deadline, and we have serious consequences. It's a very difficult thing for me, who has spent a lifetime in our industry and a good part of which is with APS, to stand before you and report that our record of 99.6 percent reliable service might be in jeopardy, despite all the sound and adequate planning to meet the needs of the people.

"But when a company has accepted a challenge and responsibility, when we have on our staff the best talents and skills available, when we have hired the leading engineering consultants and contractors to build pollution control systems, and when we have had our equipment designed and manufactured by the blue ribbon manufacturers of America, when we have used skilled craftsmen and workmen to do the job, and when our attitude has been to meet all regulations, and then surpass them, when we have spent every dollar that could be reasonably expected to provide the best system, then I don't know what else could be expected of us."

Reilly's plea for understanding comes a bit late for those aware of APS' history on pollution. The fact is, APS would never have installed equipment if it hadn't been ordered to do so by federal officials. And problems with the existing equipment are a result not of environmental campaigns or pollution technology, but cost-cutting and lack of concern on the part of management.

The utilities have not spent enough money to try to develop better abatement equipment because they have never really bothered to plan ahead to curb pollution. They complain that pollution laws change too rapidly, creating what is known in the industry as a "moving target" of regulations that get stricter and stricter, causing more expense. Yet they are able to plan ahead to accommodate "moving" power growth. The utilities, instead of trying to forecast and control increased pollution, actively fight pollution regulations, as is evident in Southern California Edison's $25,000 contribution to a campaign which resulted in the 1972 defeat of Proposition Nine, a California environmental protection initiative.

The utilities have demonstrated that if they are left alone to regulate themselves "in a reasoned and prudent manner," they will never get the job done. If they are allowed, with the acquiescence of the federal government, to determine whether the cost of abatement is worth the benefits to the environment, the equipment will not be installed—to their benefit and our cost. Meanwhile, the pollution spewing and dripping forth daily from Four Corners and Mojave does not augur well for the people of the United States.

FOUR

⊒⊨ AIR

It's terrible when they work. Since they
started, people began to change. The air began
to change. It is something we have not known
before. The plants seem to have no life. When
the wind blows our way, the coal dust covers
the whole ground, the food, the animals, the
hogans, the water. The dust is dirty, it is black.
The sun rises, it is gray. The sun sets, yet it is
still gray. I imagine the night is gray.

(Ted Yazzie, Navajo
living on Black Mesa)

Pollution is not only an aesthetic problem. The skies darken, visibility is reduced, and people die—not for lack of scenery, but because they breathe in tiny particles of ash, mixed with oxides of sulfur and nitrogen that billow from cars, factories, and power-generating plants.

When the question "who pollutes?" is raised, utilities executives point the finger at car manufacturers or steel mills and begin quoting statistics. They inform the public that power plants contribute only 14 percent of the nation's air pollution. But they neglect to mention that that 14 percent represents only the utilities' donation to particulate emissions, and

Cholla plant

that according to Federal Power Commissioner Lawrence O'Connor, power plants contribute 81 percent of the nation's sulfur oxide emissions along with other industrial sources, and over 25 percent of the nation's emissions of nitrogen oxides.

Coal-fired power plants are very inefficient systems, operating at about 40 percent efficiency. This means that if they burn 100 tons of coal, 40 tons of coal comes out as electrical power and 60 tons is lost in heat, which warms the environment in the vicinity of the power plant. Other heat losses occur in the transmission of power through the transmission lines, making the operation about 30 to 32 percent efficient.

Most emissions that come from coal-burning power plants are particulates, or ash, and sulfur dioxide and oxides of nitrogen, which are released through the combustion process when nitrogen mixes with oxygen at high temperature. Other elements, called trace elements, are released in smaller quantities. One of the most harmful of these is mercury, which is contained in coal and leaves the plant in the form of mercury vapor. Radioactive elements are also a by-product of the combustion process.

The coal burned in the Four Corners Region is of the low-sulfur variety found in the West. It contains from .05 to .08 percent sulfur, as compared with Eastern coals, which contain up to 3 percent sulfur. The ash content of the coal is considerably higher than the sulfur content—about 22 percent at Four Corners, and between 8 and 13 percent at Black Mesa (the utilities and Peabody Coal prefer the 8 percent figure, while environmentalists and noncompany scientists say the 13 percent figure is more accurate).

Whether the accepted figure is 22, 8, or 13, one thing is certain—the plants will emit thousands of tons of gases and ash each year. As the plants are all in the same air and water basin, the pollution will settle over the region, replenished each day from the millions of tons of coal burned (Dr. Shannon Robinson, of the Department of Geology at the University of New Mexico, has estimated that the six plants will burn a total of 54,531,000 tons of coal per year). And the quanti-

ties of emissions will escalate as each new plant or unit is completed.

The utilities and the Department of the Interior have generally dealt with the emissions problem by isolating the effects of *each* plant, rather than considering the cumulative effect of all six plants on the ecology and inhabitants of the region. The claim echoed and reechoed plant by plant, utility by utility, is that "there will be little effect on the ecology of the region." This is not quite the case, even on a plant-by-plant basis, as has been pointed out by the Department of Interior's *Southwest Energy Study* in the sections contributed by the Environmental Protection Agency and the National Park Service.

When Kaiparowitz is added to the five other plants in the 1980's, pollution estimates from the EPA's section of the Study project that per day about 90.4 tons of particulates, 990 tons of sulfur dioxide, and 759 tons of nitrogen oxides will be released. These estimates are based on the understanding that plants will have installed state-of-the-art pollution abatement equipment. If that equipment works as inefficiently as does the equipment at Four Corners, the emissions will be considerably higher. Dr. Michael Williams, Research Co-ordinator at the John Muir Institute for Environmental Studies at the University of New Mexico, estimates that fly ash emissions will be 240 per day, with 2,119 tons of sulfur dioxide and 850 to 1300 tons of oxides of nitrogen. Again, no matter whom one chooses to believe, the

Four Corners plant

figures are appalling. According to the Los Angeles County Air Pollution Control District's *Profile of Air Pollution* for 1971, in the Los Angeles Basin, the most notoriously polluted area in the country, 130 tons of particulates per day were emitted, with 250 tons of SO_2 and 1,050 tons of nitrogen oxides. This was from all industrial sources. Yet the EPA estimates that Kaiparowitz alone will produce 405.8 tons of emissions per day, including 210 tons of SO_2.

Fred Binnewils, of Page (Arizona) Citizens for Best Environment, speaking at Congressional Hearings on power production in the Southwest, quoted data from scientists at the Los Alamos Scientific Laboratory, who say that under the best conditions, that is, with the best abatement equipment, visibility in the area, at present more than 100 miles, will be reduced by 50 percent. But the most important and damaging effects will be on the health of people, animals, and terrestrial and aquatic plants in the area.

Particulates are well known to city dwellers. It's the stuff that makes your face grimmy after walking for an hour in New York or Los Angeles. But it does more than dirty the face. Where high particulate concentrations are found, studies report higher incidence of cancer of the stomach, esophagus, prostate, bladder, and lungs. The most harmful particulates are called "fines," very tiny particles that are hard to trap in abatement equipment. Present attempts at pollution control in plants like Four Corners have not been successful at weeding out these particles in between 0.5 and 0.01 micron in size, mainly because to do so requires more expensive equipment.

The second most common ingredient in power plant pollution is no less toxic than particulates. Dr. John Holdren of the California Institute of Technology explained in his book *Energy* some of the more potent powers of sulfur dioxide:

> The oxides of sulfur are considered the most dangerous of the air pollutants listed. They are implicated in rising death rates from bronchitis, emphysema, lung cancer, and other respiratory ailments. Adverse effects to health are thought to be possible at sulfur dioxide, SO_2, concentrations as low as 0.04 parts per million.
>
> The oxides of sulfur have the particularly insidious property of interacting synergistically with particulate matter; the combined effect of the two contaminants when both are present exceeds the sum of the effects that would be experienced if they acted independently.

At Fruitland, New Mexico, National Air Pollution Control Agency calculations say half-hour peak concentrations are often as high as two parts per million—or fifty times higher than the figure cited by Dr. Holdren as potentially harmful. When the WEST grid is complete this figure will increase exponentially. Sulfur oxides also mix with water, to form sulfuric acid, causing sulfuric acid rains, which, as one might suppose, are extremely harmful to plant and animal life.

Oxides of sulfur took the lives of 4,000 Londoners in the Killer Smog of 1952, and again the lives of more than 100 New Yorkers in 1967, when temperature inversions, warm air moving in over a cold air surface, preventing normal movement of air currents,

held smog over those cities like an electric blanket refusing to shut off.* Deaths from the East Coast inversion during the summer of 1972 are still being counted.

Leonard O. Myrup, a professor of Meteorology at the University of California, testified at the 1971 Congressional hearings that the Southwest has the highest instance of low-level temperature inversions (500 feet or lower) in the entire country. "Low level inversions occur about 55 percent of the time in winter and 40 percent of the time in summer. This data suggests that the Southwest region may be the worst area in the United States to locate polluting industries. The high frequency of low-level inversion layers at night means that during these hours the plume of pollution will not disperse. Instead, it will maintain high concentrations and drift with the wind for many miles."

Sulfur dioxide does indeed color the night—with poison. Yet David Fogarty, of SCE, stated that his company has no sulfur removal equipment at any of its plants and although they are experimenting on some removal processes at Mojave, according to Fogarty's comments, their heart really isn't in it. "We're not convinced," he explained, "that we need to remove the sulfur from our stacks because we don't think they have any detrimental effects. We think ground level concentration is negligible."

* John C. Esposito, *Vanishing Air: Nader Study Group Report on Air Pollution.*

The concentrations may be negligible in Fogarty's Los Angeles office, but they may not be so negligible to the inhabitants of the Southwest, who will breathe the gases and water their crops with sulfuric acid rains. Coupled with nitrogen oxides, NO_x, the effect of SO_2 can be disastrous. When NO_x combines with SO_2, it causes injury to plant life and human health. Howard P. Allen of SCE testified that NO_x and SO_2 standards can be met, despite conflicting evidence, partly because there are few other polluting industries in the Southwest and few cars. He does not take into consideration what effect planned urbanization will cause, when factories and cars move into the area. Nor does he consider the effect thirty or more other power-generating plants will have.

One of the most dangerous emissions from the plants will be mercury vapor. It is hard to calculate exactly how much mercury the plants will release, but the EPA has estimated that from Four Corners alone, between 1963 and 1970, from 0.219 to 0.438 tons of mercury could have passed over the Navajo Lake Watershed, with much settling in the lake itself. Colorado and New Mexico officials have already reported mercury levels in fish from the Lake as high as 0.9 ppm (the Food and Drug Administration's safe level for mercury in fish is 0.5 ppm, a level critics say is much too lax).

The amount of mercury deposited in the Navajo Lake may seem trivial, but mercury is a very toxic substance, in very small quantities. The effects of mercury poisoning have recently resounded through the international community, and in the United States have achieved the proportions of a national scandal, due to the failure of the government to deal adequately with the potential health effects of mercury.

Mercury reaches human beings and animals through the disposal of industrial wastes and through the respiration of mercury vapor from power

KATHLEEN KERSHAW

Fish from Morgan Lake,
Four Corners

plants, among other sources. Microorganisms in aquatic environments metabolize mercury and mercury compounds into the highly lethal poison methyl mercury. Methyl Mercury is then ingested by fish that eat these organisms, and the fish are then ingested by humans and animals. With each step in this food chain, the methyl mercury is concentrated in larger and larger amounts, presenting an increasing health hazard.

Methyl mercury poisoning is a particularly insidious affliction, for which there is no known antidote. Its most renowned effects were first noted among felt-hat workers at the turn of the century, whose strange conduct coined the phrase "mad as a hatter." The symptoms of mercury poisoning begin with numbness in fingers, toes and mouth, and constriction of vision, and escalate to blindness, deafness, ravings, permanent damage to brain cells and the central nervous system and death. Scientists believe that mercury poisoning can also result in destruction of chromosomes and genetic defects, and such birth defects as idiocy and severe mental retardation in the children of mothers who have ingested contaminated food. Methyl mercury furthermore remains active in the aquatic environment for between 10 and 100 years and is slow to be excreted in humans. It is therefore known as a cumulative poison.*

Speaking on the dangers of mercury emissions at the Congressional hearings in the Southwest, J. Calvin Gittings, professor of Chemistry at the University of Utah, estimated that at one part per million of mercury, Kaiparowitz will release fifteen tons of mercury each year and that Huntington Canyon will give off from four to six tons per year. If this is so, then Utah

* Gunnar Birke, M.D. et al., "Studies on Humans Exposed to Methyl Mercury Through Fish Consumption," *Arch Environment Health*, Vol. 25, Aug. 1972.

Katherine and Peter Montague, *Mercury*, Sierra Club, 1971.

Lake, near Huntington Canyon, would receive mercury fallout, and it is possible mercury fallout would be deposited in Lake Powell.

"It is most probable," Gittings said, "that as mercury vapor reaches the cooler atmosphere it gradually absorbs and adheres to particulate matter in air. Much of it would then rain down on the surrounding countryside. Here it would, from available evidence, work its way into streams and lakes. At this stage the conversion to methyl mercury occurs through biological activity. This dangerous substance then concentrates in tissues of fish and other living organisms. The magnitude of danger is difficult to estimate. However, the danger is not negligible, and it may be very serious. . . .

"Perhaps of greater concern is the fact that the world's worst mercury poisoning, leaving over forty dead and many more disabled, was traced to fish from a polluted body of water, Minamata Bay, Japan. There mercury was present at 1.6 to 3.6 parts per billion, not significantly above our tentative value for Utah Lake."

Mercury poisoning is not a pleasant ailment. Victims suffer motor defects resembling Parkinson's Disease, and death can result.

The EPA's part of the *Southwest Energy Study* confirms possible dangers of mercury and other trace elements. The study says that

insufficient information currently exists with which to quantify specific health effects. However, it

should be pointed out that the ones [trace elements] marked offer potential for deleterious effects on human health and some ecosystems. It is crucial that detailed studies be carried out as soon as possible of postulated health and ecological effects. *Until such information is developed, it should be recognized that trace element quantities may well increase pollutant burdens in human tissues, alter human physi-*

Four Corners plant

ology, and even induce, accelerate or aggravate dangerous chronic disorders including heart disease, renal disease, lung disease and cancer. Of special concern is the accumulation of trace elements in dustfall and in and around households and inhabited areas." (our emphasis)

The Study, which deals only with plants on government or Indian land, and only within a limited region, goes

on to explain that the plants will have "significant impact on terrestrial biota and water quality," and that "the combined operation of the Navajo and proposed Kaiparowitz plants can be expected to have a dramatic effect in nearby canyons of the Colorado River." In comments criticizing the *Southwest Energy Study* as a whole, EPA voiced its opposition to siting of the plants, which the comments said will affect scenic resources and visibility, especially in cases where plants are located close together, as are Kaiparowitz and Navajo, and San Juan and Four Corners.

Yet the utilities continue to assert that the Southwest is a "big country," so big that cumulative effects from the plants will be nil. And executives like M. C. Titus, executive vice-president of APS, insist that "We are confident that any ecological effects will be so slight as to be unmeasurable."

It's nice to know the utilities can maintain such unshakable confidence, despite the very shaky evidence that backs it up.

But again, the utilities are speaking relatively, and their judgments are based on cost-benefit analyses. They are giving the Indians very little and taking advantage of the impoverished state of most Indians to proclaim that the revenues are worth any cost to the tribes. One doubts, had the Tribal Councils been given all the facts about environmental ills, that they would have given their approval to the deal.

The Department of the Interior, in contracts negotiated for the plants, has manifested its concern for the health and welfare of its wards. That concern is slanted—in the direction of the utilities. Contracts for the plants require that electrostatic precipitators (used for particulate removal) operate at 97 percent efficiency, and that they be checked only every ten years. There are no stipulations concerning SO_2 and NO_x removal in the contracts. In a letter from the Assistant Commissioner for Standards and Compliance of the National Air Pollution Control Administration to the District Health Officer of Clark County, Nevada, William H. Meggonell voiced NAPCA's objections to the contracts.

"This is to inform you," the letter reads, "that NAPCA was *not* consulted regarding contract language, and we do not agree with it and our objections have been made known to the Department of the Interior. Specifically we do not agree with percentage-removal efficiency specification. . . . Further we do not agree that 97 percent efficiency reflects either current state-of-the-art electrostatic precipitator technology or the technology extant when the contract was being negotiated, and we believe that the most effective control available should be utilized to protect and preserve air quality in the recreational areas surrounding the Mojave and other plants in the Southwest."

In 1969, the NAPCA did not believe plants were being installed with state-of-the-art abatement equipment; and in 1973 many experts still believe that equipment being installed is not as effective as it could and should be.

All the plants in the Four Corners Region have been or will be installed with electrostatic precipitators (equipment that charges particles of ash and collects them on collection plates). The utilities claim that design efficiency past 99.5 percent will be difficult, if not impossible, to attain. Department of Health, Education and Welfare estimates quoted by Dr. John Bartlitt of the Los Alamos Scientific Laboratory, in his testimony at Congressional Hearings in 1971, insist that a design efficiency of 99.7 to 99.9 percent is not only possible, but has been achieved, in countries like Germany, on low-sulfur coal similar to coals found in the Southwest.

The utilities are also working with wet scrubbers (mechanisms that collect particles and trap them in a liquid film) for particulate removal. But they are not doing much to install and perfect the most efficient system for reducing particulates, especially particles from 0.5 to 0.001 micron in size, which cause the greatest reduction in visibility and harm to human health. These are bag-house filters, which collect particles in a filtering mechanism.

"Bag filters work more efficiently on fine particles than do electrostatic precipitators," Dr. Bartlitt said. "Bag filters are another example of available technology which could be, but is not being applied. Bag filters of over 99.9 percent efficiency could be designed and would allow only one-sixth as much pollution as a 99.4 percent unit and one-thirtieth as much as a 97 percent unit. This represents a difference of *200 tons* of fly ash in the air per day." (our emphasis)

In NO_x and SO_2 abatement, the area in which they are one of the primary polluters, the utilities claim that there are no proven control systems available. This is in part due to the lackadaisical attitude of the utilities in developing such systems. Some sulfur is being removed with wet scrubbers. Southern California Edison, the Salt River Project and Arizona Public Service are working on a project at Mojave to experiment with various sulfur removal processes. The project began, however, after the plant had already choked the air with tons of sulfur dioxide, rather than during the ten-year lead time in which the plant was being planned and constructed. Further attempts at NO_x and SO_2 removal, the utilities say, are reflected in high stack heights, which in reality do nothing to remove the gases but simply disperse them at higher elevations. And then there are some attempts at modifying the combustion process to try to reduce nitrogen oxide emissions.

Some engineering experts maintain that when the utilities say there are no proven means of sulfur removal, they are exaggerating. Dr. Noel de Nevers, Associate Dean of Engineering at the University of Utah, told the Committee on Interior and Insular Affairs hearings that, "One must understand that when the utilities say 'no proven technology' they do not mean the same thing that the public understands by those words. The

Near Black Mesa

public construes those words to mean that the engineers could not now design and build a reliable and effective sulfur dioxide removal scheme. The industry spokesmen really mean that there is no method available to them which would accomplish that result at a price they are willing to pay.

"In the 1930's in Great Britain, two major power plants had stack gas scrubbing systems for the removal of sulfur oxides. These were highly efficient, recovering up to 98 percent removal of sulfur oxides. These were not pilot plants; they operated on large power plants, comparable in size to those in many American cities. These units were designed on a crash basis, when the sulfur oxide problem seemed most severe.They had some operating difficulties, but they were successfully operated for numerous years."

For minor additional cost, de Nevers added, those systems operating in England were successful at removing nitrogen oxides, which the utilities say are even more difficult to remove than sulfur oxides; and for which no removal technology, they insist, exists today. But if no technology really means "it's too expensive and we don't want to spend the money," then one must be skeptical of utilities' claims that they cannot, presently, or in the near future, remove stack gases and trace elements.

Again, it is all a question of money. When M.C. Titus of APS was asked to delineate that company's commitment to sulfur removal, he answered that the company was committed to 80 percent sulfur removal, if it seems "practical" to them. But the utilities do not measure practicality in terms of disease and death, but rather in dollars and cents. They complain that they

San Juan plant

might have to spend $50 million on abatement equipment at a plant like Kaiparowitz, yet the entire plant, including transmission lines, will cost almost one and a half *billion* dollars, which means that pollution control would take up only a fraction of its cost. Besides, it is eminently practical to control pollution. *The Nader Study Group Report on Air Pollution,* for example, estimated that damages caused by pollution from all sources in the United States have cost the country between $10 and $15 billion dollars in property damage per year.

In a press release dated April 1, 1971, Federal Power Commissioner Lawrence J. O'Connor stated that all forms of pollution could be, in the future, removed from power plant stacks for an added 25 percent in cost of power. These costs could be defrayed from the average consumer by making costs higher to industry. Or costs could further be defrayed by government contributions to pollution control. That is, if the government could make as much of a commitment to preserving the environment as it now makes to waging useless wars and destroying air, land, and water both here and in foreign countries.

The government's actions, however, indicate no willingness to make such a commitment or to reassess its support for the plants. Despite severe criticism of Interior's *Southwest Energy Study* on the part of the EPA, whose critical comments contend that the study is not adequately representative of the information collected by the various work groups that contributed to it, and that it did not fully treat adverse effects on aesthetic values and air pollution and water pollution, Interior seems unfailing in its backing of WEST. The Department has disregarded the evidence of its own study and concludes in its draft summary of the study that there are no alternatives to the plants; and that if the public wants power, it will have to make some "environmental trade-offs." That such "trade-offs" severely reduce the standard of living the power plants are supposed to increase is an issue that is rarely discussed.

In a Report of the Committee on Interior and Insular Affairs, released in the summer of 1972, further criticism was leveled at the projected plants and mines, again illuminating Interior's failure to protect the environment. The report states that:

The present Four Corners situation reflects the cumulative effect

of numerous resource management decisions, each of which was limited in the scope of its objectives, and of its geographic concern. Private and public utilities, local, State, and Federal agencies, Indian tribes, corporations and individuals collectively and severally have participated in decisions which were made to achieve limited and relatively short-term goals and which were often made without full knowledge or adequate consideration of the full range of alternatives, the potential regional impacts, or the long-range desirability of the actions involved.

In 1968, for example, the Congress in accordance with a recom-

mendation of the Executive Branch authorized the Secretary of the Interior to become a financial participant in the Navajo thermal power plant. This participation was viewed as an attractive alternative to the construction of major hydroelectric dams on the Colorado River primarily because of environmental opposition to the dams. The long-term environmental impact of the thermal-electric alternatives, however, was not subjected to study in detail equivalent to the dams.

This and other single objective decisions have resulted in investments of natural resources and commitments to courses of action which will seriously constrain the remaining opportunities to achieve optimum resource and environmental management throughout the region.

The utilities and the federal government have shown that their main interest is to placate the public with promises studded with impressive statistics and studies that have no effect on previously established policies. They are unwilling, however, to supply the money and staff to fulfill their promises by creating significant abatement and research programs that would provide alternatives to the present situation. Maybe the utilities will even throw in a free gas mask for each new owner of an all-electric home.

FIVE

⪢⪡ EARTH

The earth is our mother. We Hopis are very concerned because it involves all of us in this country. Once we start tearing up our mother's heart, bad things will happen. We may poke her body, her feet, all over, but when we start poking her heart, there's going to be a big convulsion, and something is going to happen. We are going to have to stop this strip mining.

(Thomas Banyaca, spokesman
for Hopi Traditionals)

Strip mining is torture to the land. Like the victims of ancient Mexican conquests, the land is flayed of its skin of vegetation and topsoil, and the spoils are exposed—the rich seams of coal. The land is blasted and devoured, until it is unrecognizable, and the conquerors move on. The land rarely recovers. Appalachia is proof of the strip miners' genius for destruction—and the Southwest is next.

The coal and utilities industries have formed a very lucrative partnership, with utilities providing the major market for coal, using strip-mined coal to fuel one third of the nation's generating plants. The strip-mining process

*Plants struggling to grow
through coal*

is an ugly one, but it is also very economical. It costs coal companies about $.50 per ton to extract strip-mined coal compared to about $2.75 for extraction of coal from underground mines. The coal companies can therefore make enormous profits, as the full costs of the enviromental damage from stripping are not part of their cost-benefit budgeting.

To mine the layers of coal, lying anywhere from 20 to 200 feet under the ground, the top covering of vegetation and soil is loosened by blasting. Then the draglines move in—huge shovels that are dragged across the earth, consuming from 36 to 180 cubic yards of overburden between their ragged metal jaws. The 85-cubic-yard-line going in at Number Two Mine on the mesa will be able to move around 8,000 tons of overburden in an hour, pushing what was once a natural ecological design into conical piles of rubble that make a rim around the coal seam that is sometimes as much as 100 feet high.

At Black Mesa, which will have the honor of being the largest strip mine in the world, 64,858 acres of land have been leased by Peabody Coal Company. The company says only 14,000 acres contain mineable coal, and they will be stripped in annual gulps of 400 acres.

The first seam of coal at the mesa is separated from the second by a six- to nine-foot shale parting, which lies over a vein from five to eight feet thick. The third vein, two to four feet thick, is in turn separated from the second by one and a half feet of parting. Peabody has a thirty-five-year lease with both the Navajo and Hopi to accomplish its evisceration of the earth, a process that will do much more than release coal.

The earth at coal mines is also layered with iron, manganese, and sulfur. All these minerals were deposited under the ground eons ago in a delicate order which is blown to bits and turned into the chaotic mess of overburden when the blasting begins. When the sulfur mixes with water from rain and snow, it turns into sulfuric acid and sodium sulfates, which can inhibit plant growth. In Appalachia, 12,000 miles of streams have been polluted by silt and chemicals released from strip mines. Now the same process is beginning in the Southwest.

Although there is light annual rainfall in the region, there are heavy snows in winter and flash floods in summer. The rain and snow catch the chemicals from the mine and carry them down the central wash in the region, the Moencopi Wash, which deposits water, mixed with thick shale mud, on the fields of the Navajo and Hopi.

Vernon Taylor, a geologist at Prescott College in Arizona, has confirmed the dangers of strip mining to Indian agriculture. "What I see on Black Mesa as potential problems," he said on an NET special on Black Mesa, "from a geologist's point of view, are twofold. The first is a matter of disintegration of the shale that is removed during the mining process. The shale, when wet, tends to disintegrate. It consists of a type of clay, a clay mineral, which hydrates pretty rapidly when wet and tends to form a thick mud.

"The second series of problems are essentially of a chemical nature. The shale and the low-grade coal piled in the spoil banks contain sulfur. This weathers fairly quickly in our Southwestern climate, to produce sodium sulfates, which are the principal salts resulting from the weathering of shale on Black Mesa. Now, if the material is allowed to get into the Moencopi Wash system, the principal drainage area in the mining area, that causes a

YOUR PUBLIC LANDS

KAIPAROWITS PLATEAU TO THE NORTH OF US 89
CONTAINS RECOVERABLE BITUMINOUS COAL RESERVES
ESTIMATED IN EXCESS OF 10 BILLION TONS. THIS
FUEL IS MINED UNDER CLOSE SURFACE PROTECTION
SUPERVISION. THE PLATEAU WAS NAMED BY THE
POWELL SURVEY IN THE 1870'S AND WAS LATER
REFERRED TO AS WILD HORSE MESA IN THE NOVELS
OF WRITER ZANE GREY.

potential hazard for Navajo and Hopi farming communities three miles down wash.''

So the rain and snow, once a blessing that continued life, with the advent of the strip mine may bring destruction and death to the crops of the Indian tribes.

William Stockton, the vice-president of public relations for Peabody Coal, says acid run-off will not occur at Black Mesa, after the company's revegetation plans are put into effect. The EPA, however, has stated that acid production in Appalachia continues to occur on "reclaimed" lands for over one hundred years. And reclamation is much easier to accomplish in Appalachia, where there is higher rainfall, than in the dry Southwest.

Because of the aridity of the area, coal dust is everywhere in the mining area, with all the resultant air and water pollution and erosion problems. The entire removal process—creation of access roads, blasting, hauling, shipping—is accompanied by whirlwinds of black dust, dispersed by frequent high winds. The photographs of the mine in Interior's summary of the *Southwest Energy Study* show neat piles of coal and contoured spoil banks sitting undisturbed under the hot sun. In reality, the mine often looks more like a scene from a desert dust storm in *Lawrence of Arabia*. An assistant manager at the mine complained that in Kayenta, a community near the site, where the majority of mine workers live, the dust storms pack coal dust into trailers and houses, defeating all insulating material. On the mesa, where seventy-eight Navajo families have their homes, coal dust covers the land, sheep herds, and water, adding to air and water pollution from the plants themselves.

The problems caused by strip mining, although not as severe as those resulting from underground mines, have received so much public attention that Peabody is stepping up its public relations efforts to counter environmental criticism aroused by the Black Mesa Mine. The controversy has been heightened by the fact that the mine is on Indian land. Delegations from the Sierra Club and other environmental groups have been invited to the mine and the Mojave Plant, in an attempt to make Peabody's operation appear to be a model of good reclamation and environmental policy.

The contracts between the company and the tribes, okayed and pushed by Interior, stipulate that the area must be returned to the tribes in good condition, "aside from the ordinary wear and tear" of the mining process. Opponents of the mine have asked who determines what "ordinary wear and tear" means. Is it the company, is it Interior, is it the Indians? So far, there have been no answers, and the lack of clarity now may allow Peabody to destroy the environment later. Ultimately, Interior is responsible, as it has made no effort to tighten contract language.

Ordinary wear and tear aside, Peabody is promising great things from its reclamation program, which, it has stated, will leave the land in better shape than before the mining started. So far, however, the results are dismal, expecially as omens for future reclamation. In 1971, for example, the company reseeded a small lot of mined land, but the seeds were planted in September. The rains had fallen in August, as they always have, and the seeding did not take. This failure could have been prevented if the company had simply asked the Indians about farming the mesa. They have known for centuries that you plant before the rains, and that if you plant after, nothing grows.

The Environmental Protection Agency, in its parts of the *Southwest Energy Study*, suggested using irrigation water to supplement moisture from rainfall on reseeded areas, but Peabody has declined to use its slurry water for such lowly agricultural purposes. But the company does use fresh water to water the roads at the mine to check the dust. All claims to the contrary, Peabody's interest in gaining maximum profit for minimal cost seems much stronger than its rhetorical interest in reclamation. It can always blame the failure of reseeding on the weather; as an assistant manager at the mine explained: "Hell, hardly anything grows in the desert anyway."

But even if Peabody's heart and money were behind the program and

John Lansa, Hopi

the weather were perfect, some geologists question the possibilities of accomplishing significant reclamation at strip mines. Because the company does not separate the top soil from the bottom soil, which is replete with salts, the soil to be reclaimed is so highly saline that it is doubtful that it can be used at all.

There are, furthermore, no stipulations in the contract concerning the time period in which reclamation takes place. The •company must reclaim the land, but they can reclaim it in the year before the contract expires or as each area is mined. The timing is crucial to the success of reclamation and combatting pollution, for according to the EPA, the longer the spoil banks are unreclaimed, the more salts and sediment are available for erosion and water pollution. The EPA has also suggested that both coal and utilities companies be required to post bonds to assure that their environmental programs be carried out. But neither the states involved nor the federal government have been anxious to do anything to annoy or delay the companies.

While Black Mesa has become the focus of the most public indignation, it is only one of three Southwestern strip mines that will service the plants in the WEST grid. A 31,000-acre leased area, the Navajo Mine, named in honor of the tribe whose land is being destroyed, is being mined by Utah International to serve the Four Corners Plant. That mine has been in operation since 1963 and the EPA says that no "reclamation program exists at the Navajo Mine" and that "the very limited experimental program conducted by Utah to determine revegetation methods is too little and too late."

Utah is also mining a 6,000-acre area to provide fuel for the San Juan Plant. To fuel the Navajo, Mojave, Four Corners, and San Juan plants, a total of 101,958 acres of land is being destroyed. Two underground mines, at Missing Canyon and Deer Creek, will provide coal for Kaiparowitz and Huntington Canyon and must be added to the toll.

And this is only the beginning. More coal will be needed to fuel other plants required to assure the continuing growth of the utilities. Coal is also being turned into natural gas in coal gasification plants. El Paso Natural Gas is currently trying to negotiate several new leases on Black Mesa for coal gasification.

For the rape of their land, the two Indian tribes are being paid about $3,-250,000 a year in lease payments. According to present schedules, this means that each Navajo will receive about $7.00 per year. But, in fact, the payment will amount to less than that. In the first place, all the money goes to Interior and stays there until the Department decides to release it. Then it is given to the Tribal Councils, the unrepresentative bodies that seem to get richer while the majority of the tribe live in abject poverty. The Indians are also paid for each ton of coal extracted from the land: they get between $.20 and $.25 a ton, while Peabody sells the coal for $4.00 a ton.

Peabody has also announced a program to rid the reservations of unemployment. The company has agreed to hire 75 percent of its mining staff from the Indian population, paying them salaries that will average around $10,000 per year. Currently there are eighty-one union employees at the mine and twenty-four managerial employees, with sixty-one Navajo working the union jobs, where the pay is less and the hazards of Black Lung disease and emphysema are the highest. Only seven of the managerial employees are Navajo, and there are no Hopi employed in any capacity. When the mine operates at full capacity, there will be three hundred jobs set aside for the Indians. Currently there are 130,000 Navajo and 6,000 Hopi on the reservations, with chronic unemployment running as high as 70 to 80 percent. When the company leaves in thirty-five years, the three hundred jobs will be terminated—along with much of the farming and sheepherding that has sustained the community for thousands of years.

Yet the mining, despite all the problems raised, has the support of both Navajo and Hopi Tribal Councils. Clarence Hamilton, Council Chairman of the Hopi, puts out glowing press releases lauding the companies and claiming that the Traditionals are troublemakers with no support in the tribe itself. Many of these press releases are written for Hamilton by a public relations firm in Salt Lake City, David W. Evans Inc., the same firm, coincidentally, that writes all the public relations for WEST.

The only problem Peter McDonald, chairman of the Navajo Tribal Council, finds with the mine is that it does not solely belong to the Navajo. "Strip mining doesn't really bother me," he commented on an NET special, "because, first of all, any resource that is on the reservation under the ground is for the Navajo to utilize. And why couldn't the tribe build these power plants and sell the power to

California, rather than just receive one tenth of what the actual economic gain is from these resources?"

Strip mining is something McDonald can tolerate because the mine is not in his backyard, and he doesn't depend on the land for sustenance. But for the Navajo families living on the mesa and tending their sheep, the mine has mainly brought chaos and destruction. Fifty-three families live directly on land that will be mined. Their hogans will be moved and the company has promised to pay for the moving and for the construction of new homes. There are, however, no provisions in the lease for remuneration for livestock lost in the process or for assuring grazing land for the sheep once the families are relocated.

Overgrazing on the mesa has always been a problem, and not one that Peabody created. But it is one that the company's operations have exacerbated. With the mining, there is much less land on which the sheep can graze, a situation which threatens the very livelihood of the majority of the Indians on the mesa. Peabody's attitude has been one of blithe unconcern for the overgrazing problem. "The overgrazing problem was there before we ever heard of it," Bill Stockton said on the NET special. "It is not our job to solve that problem."

The Indians seem to have no recourse against the machines that are not only tearing away coal from the land, but tearing at the very fabric of their lives, woven from the earth, colored by the roots and shrubs, and pieced together in a very delicate and precarious balance. Most did not choose their poverty and would be glad for improvement. But improvement is not what Peabody or the utilities are offering.

Despite all the sincere pleas of concern for the Indians, individual members of both tribes have complained that their dealings with representatives of some utilities and coal companies have been marked not with understanding but with deception. The State of New Mexico, in response to Indian complaints, filed suit against the Tucson Gas and Electric Company and its agent, Coats Field Service, for fraudulently purchasing agreements granting permission for rights of way for transmission lines. The Attorney General's office later decided not to pursue the case.

Currently, a campaign is being waged in Congress to further weaken the Indians' ability to fight the mining of the land. Parts of the Black Mesa Mine are on land that is jointly used by Hopi and Navajo. The issue of ownership of Black Mesa has been contested for years by the two tribes, each claiming full ownership. Traditionals prefer to attempt continued joint use, rather than settle the dispute through the U.S. judicial system. The white man, in the person of Arizona Congressman Sam Steiger, is unhappy with this solution and has put forth a bill in Congress that would partition the joint-use area. The main and most convenient effect of this action would be to place the mine solely in Navajo hands, thus diluting the opposition to Peabody. For it is the Hopi who have been the most outspoken in their opposition to the mine and have filed suit in federal court to try to halt the mining. Should the mine be stopped, Arizona would lose over half a billion dollars in tax revenues, which may explain Steiger's action.

The Indians have become the symbolic sacrificial victims in a struggle that reaches beyond the boundaries of the desert in the great Southwest. Land is one of our most important national assets. In our reckless haste to "use" it all now we ultimately betray ourselves: a betrayal that benefits a few privileged persons and corporations to the great detriment of us all.

SIX
∃∈
WATER

The desert is a house made of dawn
A house made of evening light.
When it rains,
Dark clouds are at the house's door.
The zigzag lightning stands high upon it.
Happily with abundant showers may I walk.
Happily with abundant plants may I walk.
(Navajo Night Chant)

Water is life in the Southwest. Measured in droplets instead of gallons, it is conserved through a natural economy in which plants, animals, and man participate, instinctively, so that the land, scaled by drought and sun, will allow growth. Industry has rarely understood this brand of economics. And all the talk of ecological systems by respected scientists seems to have little effect. Each day, 2,700 gallons of water per minute are pumped from under the ground on Black Mesa and used to ship coal. Each year, over 200,-000 acre-feet of water from the Colorado River and its tributaries are stored and polluted by power plants, while the land and Indians of the Southwest parch and wither.

The Black Mesa Mine is 275 miles

Four Corners plant

from the power plant it fuels. To get coal to the plant an enormous pipeline was built in which the coal is pulverized and mixed with water and· pumped across the desert to Mojave. The pipeline can swallow up to 43,000 tons of slurried coal per day and will consume anywhere from 37 to 39 *billion* gallons of water in thirty-five years. The water Peabody uses to annoint and ship its coal comes from five wells that have been sunk over 3,000 feet under the ground into the Navajo sandstone aquifer (an aquifer is a subsurface water-bearing rock formation), the main aquifer for groundwater in the region. It is fossil water—deposited eons ago. Many surface springs in the area are also fed from this aquifer of clear, unpolluted water that cannot be replaced. Once rich in

Mojave plant water supply

rainfall, the region gets only between six and fifteen inches of rain a year, in a good year.

Because of the folds and faults in the earth, the aquifer is far beneath the surface around Black Mesa, and the Indians draw their water from water-bearing layers closer to the surface. Relative to the area around it, the mesa is a structural basin; drawing vast quantities of water from beneath the mesa, therefore, will probably not affect the water table for the people there. But for the people on the rim of the basin, times ahead will be dry, as water, including subsurface water, flows downhill to replace losses.

In a letter to the National Park Service, E. H. McGovack, of the Water Resources Division of the United States Geological Survey, emphasized the effect pumping could have on the water table in the area. "The U.S. Geological Survey has made some preliminary calculations of the long-term effect of the Peabody Coal Company well field on groundwater supplied in the Black Mesa area," he wrote. "We expect the water table to be lowered about 100 feet at Kayenta [north of the mesa] over a 30-year period, and lesser water level declines should occur at several other communities near Black Mesa."

Peabody has assured the tribes that Indian water on the mesa will not be reduced by pumping, and it has encased their wells to prevent seepage. It has not, however, dealt with the question of lowering of the water table in neighboring communities. The lease between the company and the tribes allows the Department of the Interior the "option" to intervene should there be an adverse effect on groundwater. The Department can require the company to deepen artesian wells in the area to supply the quantity and quality of water formerly available, or it can require the company to provide water for slurry from another source that "will not significantly affect the supply of groundwater in the vicinity."

Again, contract language is crucial. The Department has the "option to intervene" but is not required to do so. And this option can be exercised when groundwater in "the vicinity" is

affected. But what is the "vicinity"? Does it include the rim of the basin, where the effects will be felt most critically? And what does Interior consider an adverse effect?

Currently, monitoring programs to determine that effect have been minimal. But even significant monitoring programs would not necessarily protect Indian water, for it would not be a *preventive* program. If Interior determined that a lowering of the water table by 100 feet was sufficient to force Peabody to secure water by other means, and monitoring programs discovered such a water reduction, that would still mean an enormous loss of water in the area, a loss that could not be recouped. Interior has not even made such a determination. And as

the Great White Father nods, Peabody goes on pumping over a million gallons a day.

Peabody is paying the Indians for the water it takes from the mesa, water that could be used to make their arid land and lives bloom if the U.S. Government were really interested in improving the conditions of its wards. The Navajo get $5.00 per acre-foot of water and the Hopi $1.75. A bargain rate, when one considers that the Central Arizona Project will sell water in the Phoenix area for $50 per acre-foot. But the government seems to think that since the Indians have done without for so long, doing without forever won't hurt.

There is just not enough water in the Southwest for coal and people. Cognizant of this, the EPA, in its "Water Pollution Report" for the *Southwest Energy Study*, proposed that Peabody dig wells that would use briny water, rather than wasting fresh water on coal. So far, nothing has been done about this suggestion.

Peabody, in its brochure "Mining on Black Mesa," has also generously agreed to fill its last mining cut with water so that it could be used as a reservoir for the Indians. But this plan seems highly impractical: strip-mined land is so full of silt and chemicals that it would pollute the water and possibly kill or damage anything it irrigated.

The water pollution problems raised by the strip mines, underground mines, and power plants are enormous. Strip mines add to water pollution when water mixes with chemicals and shale from spoil banks. Underground mines leach chemicals from mined areas and ash disposal areas. And power plants contribute to water pollution in myriad ways, from consumption of valuable water, to thermal and chemical pollution released in the generating and cooling processes.

The EPA, in the *Southwest Energy Study*, notes that, "The operation of fossil-fueled power plants may cause water pollution from the following sources: condenser cooling systems (waste heat and chemicals), boiler-fed water treatment operations (waste chemicals), plant system cleaning water (waste chemicals), exhaust treatment system (liquid wet scrubber effluents), and solid waste handling systems (ash slurry water). In addition, stack emissions may have a substantial impact on the water environment."

Four Corners will have the most substantial impact on water pollution. The plant gets its water from the San Juan River, from which it draws 51,000 acre-feet per year (16,618,401,000 gallons). The plant uses a cooling pond, called Morgan Lake, which is periodically flushed out, with water flowing down the Chaco Wash into the San Juan River. This "blowdown" water is replete with chemicals and dissolved solids, all of which are carried into the river. This flushing water can also cause thermal (heat) pollution. Further pollution comes from ash disposal sites, where bottom ash is placed in settling ponds. The water from these ponds can overflow, again re-

Near a Hopi village

turning to the San Juan, which is a tributary of the Colorado.

The other plants in the grid have taken more preventive water pollution measures. Nevertheless, all present water hazards. Mojave, for instance, is allowed to return some water to the Colorado and is thus considered a potential pollution source by the EPA. The plants use cooling towers to cool water, and waste water from most of the plants, other than Four Corners, goes into evaporation ponds, where the chemicals and solids settle out. Sudden rains can cause evaporation ponds and cooling towers to overflow, however, and chemicals have leached out of ash disposal sites, ending up back in the river water as a source of water pollution. And stack emissions do not stay suspended in the air, but eventually fall to the ground, creating still more water pollution.

It takes an enormous amount of water to run a power plant. About 300,000 acre-feet of water per year from the Colorado and its tributaries has been set aside for use in the six plants. Kaiparowitz alone will use 102,200 acre-feet per year—or enough water to meet the needs of the entire city and county of San Francisco for one year. The Mojave Plant will use 30,000 acre-feet, which is 10 percent of all the water allocated to the State of Nevada under the Supreme Court Decree of 1963 defining the Colorado River Compact. Nevada now has 380,000 acre-feet available to

it. But by the year 2000, it is estimated that the state will need 500,000 acre-feet to meet increasing population. With 30,000 acre-feet going to Mojave, and still more to other proposed plants in the area, Nevada may not be able to provide water to its people, though the power plants will be drinking steadily.

The same water shortage problem has been projected for the State of Utah. Senator Frank Moss has testified that Utah will soon be out of water. Despite this shortage, applications for water for fourteen other 1,000-MW power plants have been filed for locations in Utah, and the Bureau of Reclamation has signed a water service contract to supply 44,000 acre-feet of water to cool a power plant the size of Four Corners in New Mexico, another state that suffers from water shortages.

The water resources of the Colorado have long been overallocated. The federal government and the utilities are well aware of this problem. Yet, they still plan escalating projects for use of the river's waters. Such projects simply mean gaining water rights from other users.

Colorado River water has long been one of the most sensitive issues in the Southwest, and between the United States and Mexico. The river has an annual flow of between 12 million and 13 and a half million acre-feet and is divided at Lee's Ferry, Arizona, into an upper and lower basin, each getting half the yearly flow. Disputes

Four Corners plant and Morgan Lake

between the states over actually getting the water out of the river have waged hot and heavy for more than forty years. At one point in the 1930's, for instance, Arizona National Guardsmen were dispatched to the east bank of the Colorado to harass Bureau of Reclamation construction of a California diversion project. More recently, Arizona fought California's claims to the water in a case which won an eleven-year hearing before the U.S. Supreme Court. To compound the difficulties, Mexico is assured of 1.5 million acre-feet of Colorado water per year. In short, everyone has plans for the Colorado's water.

The Four Corners Regional Development Commission talks of building a metropolis in the area—a metropolis that will need water. Phoenix and Tucson are expanding rapidly and have no desire to stop expanding, or to curtail their growing water needs. The Bureau of Land Management has set aside land near the Mojave Plant for an urban area, without telling anyone where the city's water will come from. Together, these plans present a picture of an enormous megapolis, stretching from Mojave to New Mexico, fueled by the utilities, thirsting for water in the desert, where there is none to be found.

To combat the water shortage problem in the Southwest, industry and the federal government have discussed numerous schemes, most of

Overleaf: John Lansa, Hopi

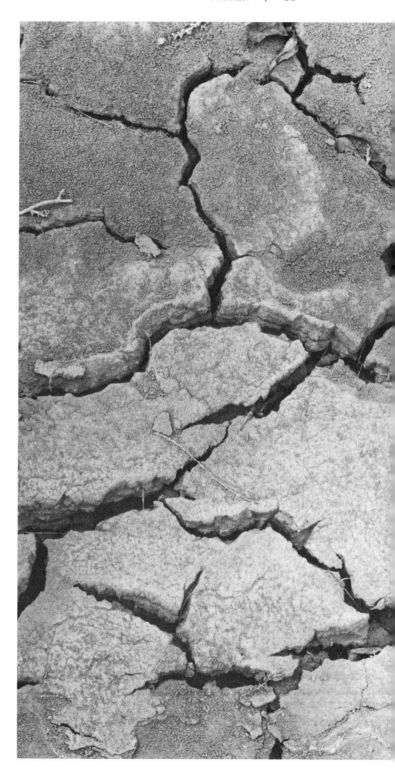

which are worthy of a Walter Mitty or a Pentagon expert returned from Indochina.

One report in the *Southwest Energy Study* on water pollution and consumption suggested unwittingly an excellent means of bringing the war home to the American public—defoliating parts of the Southwest. Because the Colorado is overallocated, and because more water is needed for industrial use, trees like aspens, found in alpine areas where there is more moisture, could be sprayed with defoliants that would reduce their moisture intake.

The same report also suggested massive changes in the fauna of the Southwest to provide water yield increases. One wonders what will happen to the multimillion-dollar tourist industry, when on top of polluted water in recreational areas, visitors are asked to suffer the effects of defoliants.

If all the above plans fall through, there is still the water that belongs to the Indians. The Westinghouse Report on a new town for the Four Corners Region provides information on how to obtain Indians' water rights. States in the area can set aside Indian water, either by purchase or condemnation, a model of which exists in the State of Colorado where there is a "constitutional acknowledgement of priorities which permits municipal users to condemn, with adequate compensation, a

Mojave plant

Mojave plant water storage

domestic or agricultural water users' right." We have already seen what adequate compensation means when it concerns paying the Indians for their water.

Under treaty and law the Navajo Indians have been given the first rights to water touching their reservation in quantities deemed necessary for "present and future use." Such expansive water rights, if continued, would have meant that the tribe would have the right to water needed for power plants. It was therefore necessary to put a limit on Navajo water use. The tribe was told by Interior, House Interior Committee Chairman Wayne Aspinall of Colorado, and

WEST that if it wanted the Navajo Plant, it would have to limit its use of Colorado River water to Arizona's upper basin allotment of 50,000 acre-feet a year, and that it would have to promise the Navajo Project 34,100 acre-feet of that 50,000. The Navajos were further asked to give the city of Page, Arizona, 3,000 acre-feet per year if the tribe was given back Antelope Point, a property it has long sought. The Tribal Council agreed to these demands, waiving its Colorado River rights for the next fifty years—an agreement whose legality is seriously questioned by Indian Lawyers.

The tribe currently uses 13,000 acre-feet of water per year. The agreement, approved by Interior, means that the tribe will have only 12,900 acre-feet at its disposal, which is not enough for present use, and will not allow the tribe any growth in population, standard of living, or industrialization. The utilities and the Department of the Interior consistently reject the idea of halting growth of industry or population in the United States, but they seem to feel that zero growth is fine for the Indians. If the selling of their water rights is representative of Interior's protection of the Indians, it would probably cost the Navajos less "to buy protection."

Again, as in all the dealings involved in providing the Southwest with the unending "benefits" of electricity and coal, the effect of getting the water to run the plants and mines is not limited to the Indians. Everyone will have a chance to suffer. Withdrawing water from the Colorado and its tributaries will increase the salinity of a river whose waters are already too salty. The use of 136,000 acre-feet of water at Kaiparowitz and Navajo, according to John A. McComb, the Southwest Representative of the Sierra Club, will cause a 4 to 5 percent increase in the salinity of river water flowing into Mexico and will have an unfortunate effect on agriculture in the Imperial Valley of California and the Mexicali Valley in Mexico. In a letter from Thomas L. Kimball, Executive Director of the National Wildlife Foundation, quoted in the Committee of Interior and Insular Affairs hearings on power production in the South-

west, the Federal Water Quality Office's estimates of the monetary effect of increased salinity of the Colorado were made known to the Secretary of the Interior. The Office estimated that each one milligram increase in salinity to the Colorado below Lake Mead causes direct and indirect economic losses of $70,000 per year, hardly a significant contribution to our standard of living.

Mexico, furthermore, is not at all excited by the prospect of increased salinity in the water it receives. For the past eleven years the subject of salts in the river has been debated between the United States and Mexico. In June of 1972, Mexico's President Luis Echeverria Alvarez, on a visit to the U.S., again complained of the matter. And things will get worse for both the people of the United States and Mexico, as more and more plants are being planned, requiring more and more water that could be used for man, not machines.

If unending growth of electrical energy is continued, the problems resulting from water pollution and wasteful uses of water may soon be unsolvable. Unless modern technology comes up with a form of life that does not need water to survive and can replace human, animal, and plant life, as we know it, with this new creation, which will have, doubtlessly, an all-electric soul, we will all parch and wither, while the transmission lines remain as a monument to industry's greed.

SEVEN

⋹⋹ MAN

Today, we, Hopi and white man come face to
face at the crossroads of our respective life.
. . . It was foretold it would be at the most
critical time in the history of mankind. Everywhere people are confused. What we decide
now and do hereafter will be the fate of our
respective people. . . . Now we are all talking
about the judgment day. . . . In the light of our
Hopi prophecy, it is going to take place here
and will be completed in the Hopi empire.

(Spokesman for the
Hopi people in 1946)

America's standard of living is de-
pendent on power—the power to determine in whose interest our resources and technology are used, for
the sake of mankind or for the sake of
corporate profit. The energy crisis in
the United States, of which the energy
crisis in the Southwest is but an example, requires that the people of the
United States answer this dilemma
very soon.

The Indians believe that to dese-
crate the earth is to wreak destruction
on all of mankind. The actions of the
utilities and coal companies in the
Southwest and scientific evidence

Zuni

would seem to confirm that belief. To
continue endless growth, endless
building of power plants, with the resultant pollution, will mean damage to
the ecological balance upon which we
all depend. Once that damage is done,
it cannot be undone.

Dr. Jerome Weingart of the Environmental Quality Laboratory of the
California Institute of Technology explained that to continue present environmental policies will result in the
fulfillment of the Hopi vision of the
apocalypse. Weingart compares the
earth to a human body. The utilities
and mining companies, along with
other industries, are hacking away at

the periphery of the body, but each wound they make affects the heart. The organism may survive each separate wound against it, but that survival will be only temporary. If the attack goes on, the heart of the earth, like the heart of a human body, will stop. It will be too late to change things then. Each plant that is built without proper emissions controls, each gash into the earth without feasible and significant reclamation, is not only an attack on the Indians of the Southwest, but an attack on us all.

The utilities are aware of this, and their escalating promotional campaign seems directly proportionate to the awareness brought about by environmentalists, who, contrary to utilities propaganda, do not create pollution, but only make the public aware of its dangers. The utilities must fight this growing awareness if they are to continue to have the freedom to determine the nation's unwritten power policy. Above all, the utilities want to avoid giving the public a say in how much power is used, how much it is sold for, and what type of technology will supply it. For that participation would mean not only significant delays in expansion plans, but a possible reassessment of exponential growth itself.

In Los Angeles, the public outcry against the participation of the Department of Water and Power in the Navajo Plant resulted in the passage of a city council resolution that could jeopardize the Department's continued partnership in the building of the plant. The resolution delineates strict environmental standards, including bonds posted to encourage the efficacy of environmental programs, assurances that sheep grazing on Black Mesa will not be affected by strip mining, air pollution standards for the plants, and water monitoring programs. All these strictures must be observed at Navajo if the city is to continue to be party to the plant contracts. Otherwise, the city may be forced to withdraw its support from the project and become a simple consumer of its power, which would mean that the utilities will have to replace the city's capital input.

As a result of this, and similar popular attacks on the industry, California utilities are seeking legislation that would further discourage public participation in power policy planning. The legislation is based on estimates of future power needs—estimates the Sierra Club insists are grossly inflated —which indicated that demand will surpass supply in the very near future. On the basis of these estimates, the companies are demanding a mandate to build plants where they want, when they want, and how they want, without any delay—that is, without the hindrance of the environmentally aware citizenry. The bill further stipulates that the state should help fund a promotional campaign to educate the public to the need for more power. This would be a direct state contribution to the advertising coffers of the utilities.

The solutions to the electrical energy crisis do not lie in attacks on those who are environmentally concerned. They lie in the creation of a national power policy based on a variety of options, from improving already available energy sources, like fossil fuels, and cutting down on wasteful uses of power, to the development of new options like solar and geothermal energy, and fusion power.

Environmental experts like Dr. Weingart suggest that such a diverse power policy will create a stability that a commitment to one power source cannot provide. "The reason why biological systems make it," he said, "in spite of tremendous environmental changes on the planet, is their huge diversity. We know that fairly complex ecosystems like forests and jungles are highly stable because they are highly diverse. There is diversity at the micro level, so there is diversity at the macro level.

"With the coming of the industrial revolution, we have restricted the number of options we have, in the name of efficiency. We're locked into the car for transportation, for housing it's ticky-tacky apartments or ticky-tacky tracts, and for energy, we've become like an agricultural mono-crop. . . . We're laying ourselves open to an enormous crisis because systems which have only a very few components are very unstable and will come crashing down very quickly. Because we don't know which energy routes will be really successful, we should develop all the options in parallel. We've got to have a very broad menu of energy options."

In spite of the present controversy over the energy crisis and growing concern about the effect of energy

KATHLEEN KERSHAW

production on the environment, the utilities have resisted the creation of such a system of diverse options. Instead, they have chosen to repeat the past and lock the nation into an energy policy again based only on one option —nuclear fission power. This situation furthers the inherent instability that comes with dependence on only one power alternative, with frequent blackouts and brownouts when the system has problems. And it adds the dangers of radioactive pollution.

Nuclear fission occurs when a radioactive material like uranium decays and throws out free particles from the atomic nucleus. If these particles hit the nuclei of other atoms, the nuclei split, creating a chain reaction, which produces the heat necessary to generate electrical energy. The amount of heat generated by this chain reaction must be carefully controlled, or the reactor can melt, and the fuel vaporize, releasing radioactive emissions into the atmosphere. Present reactors are called "water-moderated reactors" because they use water to slow down the chain reaction. These reactors also consume more fissionable material than they produce.

To increase the amount of fissionable material produced in the reactor, research is being done on the liquid metal "fast breeder" reactor. Liquid sodium is used to moderate the reaction, which increases the production of fissionable material, plutonium, by concentrating it in a smaller volume, operating at higher temperatures.

The Atomic Energy Commission (AEC) has the contradictory task of both promoting and regulating uses of the atom. Both the AEC and the utilities claim that fission power represents the best alternative to the pollution of fossil-fueled power plants. Other scientists say, however, that fission power presents many dangers to the American public from possible radioactive pollution.

Two of the most vocal opponents of fission power have been Dr. John W. Goffman and Dr. Arthur R. Tamplin of the Lawrence Radiation Laboratory of Livermore, California—authors of a book condemning nuclear power plants, *Poisoned Power: The Case Against Nuclear Power Plants*. Goffman and Tamplin insist that fission represents an enormous threat to the health and welfare of Americans. They say that plants powered by nuclear fission will emit radioactive pollutants based on standards of "safe limits" set by the AEC, standards they consider much too lax. They say there is absolutely no "safe level" of radiation, that all radiation damages in some way and to some degree. Doses of radiation at the AEC's safe level, according to Goffman and Tamplin, could cause severe health and genetic defects.

The two scientists believe that nuclear power is a massive experiment that could increase the cancer and leukemia death rate and cause genetic defects, plus creating a black market in plutonium—the most dangerous poison known to man and the major ingredient in atom bombs. Furthermore, the dangers from radioactive pollution come in all phases of the power generation process, from the mining of uranium, to the disposal of radioactive wastes in vaults that must be secure for centuries, as the half-life of plutonium is 24,000 years. In short, they believe the risks of employing fission power far outweigh the benefits of use.

Dr. John Holdren of the California Institute of Technology is perhaps a less vehement critic of fission power but also points to its many problems: that despite all the stringent fail-safe devices designed to prevent accidents, such accidents could occur and would have devastating effects. "The AEC projections for the production of nuclear power," Holdren writes in his book *Energy,* "would require about 1,000 reactors in operation in 1990, which means that if the accident probability were one per 1,000 reactor years, we could then expect one accident somewhere in the United States *every year.*

"Again," he continues, "no one knows what the chance of a major accident actually is, and reassurances that cite very tiny probabilities must be taken with a grain of salt. Highly improbable events have a way of happening anyway in complicated technological systems, as the 1965 Northeast power blackout, and the sinking of the 'unsinkable *Titanic*' and the failure of other 'fail-safe' and 'fool-

proof' systems have demonstrated. . . . Can engineers who are unable to guarantee a freeway overpass against failure in a moderate earthquake guarantee a reactor building against failure in a larger one?"

Holdren, as well as Goffman and Tamplin, suggests that the American public should be allowed some say in the decision-making process that will bring fission power, as it is the American public that will take the risks involved in a nuclear accident—risks, incidentally, for which American insurance companies have refused to insure for more than one percent of the potential damages.

Yet the AEC and the utilities claim that fission power is almost totally safe and that accidents are almost impossible. They say they believe that its benefits outweigh any possible risks, and that the building of nuclear plants should continue without delay. But their seemingly blind optimism regarding fission power and their credibility record with fossil fuel does not encourage faith in their decisions.

David Fogarty, of Southern California Edison, recently reflected the kind of unquestioning support of fission that has caused skepticism in certain segments of the public. "I think when they [environmentalists] talk about the likelihood of accidents in plants," he said, "they are being unrealistic . . . I am sure there is no basis for concern. If we had a tidal wave off the coast of California, and it were 50 or 60 feet high, it would destroy the

San Onofre nuclear plant. There would be radioactive releases if the plant was operating. Now if you hypothesize that kind of tidal wave and the destruction of San Onofre and radioactive releases, you could then hypothesize that there would be maybe 10,000 deaths from those releases. But if there was a 50-foot tidal wave (now, that's never happened and it's never going to happen), you'd probably have two million people drowned off the coast of California by that same tidal wave. So the mechanism you hypothesize that would cause nuclear release would have consequences that would be enormously greater in the general public."

Fogarty picked a hypothetical situation to illustrate the small dangers involved in nuclear plants. That example, however, revealed the industry's cavalier attitude toward these dangers, and the omission of certain significant facts that seems to characterize the defense of their policies. What Fogarty neglected to mention is that a tidal wave causes incredible damage, but that the damage finishes when the tidal wave sweeps away. The radioactive emissions from a nuclear power plant disaster, by contrast, linger on for thousands of years, causing extensive damage to life and property. It is this kind of failure to include all the facts that is interwoven with the utilities' dealings with the public.

Nuclear fission power is a means by which the utilities can continue growth without being bound by the supply of coal or natural gas. Fission must therefore be staunchly defended. Rather than developing over-enthusiastic arguments to justify fission power, the utilities, with the support of the government, should be developing other nonpolluting energy options, while reducing some of the wasteful uses of power that make the energy crisis so immediate.

Unlimited growth allows for no distinction between need and extravagance, between uses of power that actually help raise the standard of living of mankind and those that contribute to its degradation. Much of the increase in power use in the past years comes precisely from applications of electrical energy that do nothing for man but degrade his environment.

One has only to travel to any large city to view the waste that the electrical utilities industry has so diligently promoted. Las Vegas uses electrical energy for lighting gambling casinos and hotel signs which require as much energy as would be needed to light hundreds of homes. Gas stations advertise with as many as three huge brightly lighted signs per station. Companies leave lights on all night to save on bulbs; incandescent rather than fluorescent lighting (which requires less power) is used in homes. Banks and other businesses which are not open at night advertise with lighted signs after dark. Aluminum cans have replaced steel, yet it takes approximately six times more energy to produce aluminum. Electric heating is slowly taking the place of gas, and some homes boast of several color

Las Vegas, Nevada

televisions and stereos all going at the same time. Buildings are poorly insulated and demand enormous heating loads, and then there is the seemingly endless proliferation of electric appliances which save the owner so little time as to be almost useless, except for their contribution to the demand for more power generation capacity.

The utilities claim that such things as electric appliances add little to their peak demand. But in a society where growth can no longer be justified in terms of any cost-benefit or environmental trade-off, all uses of power should be carefully evaluated. Why permit the expansion of energy-intensive industries, like aluminum, when, for example, steel could and should be recycled to meet much of our need?

Demand estimates, due to such wasteful uses of power, become self-fulfilling prophecies. Companies promote the unnecessary use of lighting

Zuni

at night to make more money and keep generators going, while each hour of operating time produces more and more thermal and chemical pollution.

The corporate leaders of our society seem to equate waste with wealth. There was once a time when ignorance of the environmental and social consequences of such waste allowed us the illusion that this brand of economic growth was good for the country. That time has come to an end. Continuation of unlimited power use is good only for the very few, who have little to do with the average American. It is time that industry cease operating on the theory that the growth of its profits will somehow percolate down to the average citizen and begin operating in a manner that *directly* benefits all Americans—by channeling its use of energy in directions that increase not only quantity of life, but quality of life.

One clean and eminently safe means to this end is from the sun. Dr. Weingart estimates that solar energy could contribute to heating and cooling of homes, heating of water, and small-scale electrical generation—all in the very near future. In ten to fifteen years, he says, solar energy would be available for large-scale electrical generation. Drs. Aden and Marjorie Mienel, speaking on an NET special on Black Mesa, stated that their research in solar energy indicates that in the Southwest the same amount of land currently used to produce electri-

Adam Clark Vroman, Hopi, 1901

cal power (including mines) could be used to produce an equal amount of solar energy, which is nonpolluting and lasts forever, while a conventional power plant has a lifetime of only about thirty-five years. Solar energy, however, has received almost no federal funding.

Weingart and others believe that geothermal energy, volcanically produced steam in the interior of the earth, also represents a significant power option. There is energy that is the equivalent to the burning of 900 trillion tons of coal in the hot core of the earth. Just the heat under the Imperial Valley could be tapped to produce from 30 to 90 percent of the country's electrical generating capacity. But, currently, a 100-MW power plant in Geysers, California, is the only application of geothermal energy in the nation.

Fusion power, the process of fusing atoms with heat, could provide a much safer form of nuclear energy than nuclear fission. The amount of heat needed to produce fusion in a controlled fashion has caused research problems, which some scientists say can be solved with adequately funded programs. But so far, funding has been directed primarily at fission research, which has received $23 billion from government and industry, while fusion has received barely one thousandth the amount, $30 million.

Jim Weaver, of the Ohio Energy Systems, states that total energy systems can be used to generate nonpolluting electrical energy. In Lexington,

Kentucky a shopping mall using a total energy system has an on-site generator fueled with natural gas. It has achieved 60 to 75 percent efficiency by using waste heat from the generating process to provide heat and air conditioning. Such systems have been blocked by propaganda and lawsuits by utilities, who do not want to lose the big sales that shopping centers, hospitals, and other large facilities represent.

Solar energy, geothermal energy, fusion, total energy systems, elimination of wasteful uses of power that would increase our reserves of natural gas—all these are viable alternatives to the present commitment to coal and fission that has become our national power policy. Yet, the Department of the Interior, in its recent decision to support the construction of more generating plants in the Southwest, has dismissed these viable alternatives—alternatives that can be achieved without harm to the Indians of the Southwest, the majority of the American people, or our environment.

The promise of abundant energy is a universally high standard of living, perhaps in a reclaimed environment. And the tragedy of our present energy crisis is not that there are no answers to it, but rather that there are so many which the "public utilities" and the government decline to explore. There may be no solution to the present crisis, however, if growth is not halted at present levels. Even nonpolluting solar energy has its limit. At continued growth rates, so much land would be needed to produce even solar energy that there would be no room for people. If growth is halted and power use carefully evaluated, we can avoid power rationing, resource exhaustion, pollution, and economic collapse. But again, the utilities reject as "absurd" the notion of curtailing power growth.

The final insult to the public comes when industry is asked to answer for the consequences of its policies. Economics then gives way to quantities of concern for the "masses," the "people" and their "needs." If companies pollute, corporate leaders say, if they manufacture unsafe products, this is not due to corporate greed, but rather to industry's speed in delivering the goods and services Americans "demand."

One soon discovers that industry and the U.S. Government have invented the needs of the American public to provide a justification for their own evils. They would have us believe we are the masters of their policies. But, in truth, we are only the scapegoat.

The utilities in WEST Associates and the coal companies began their plans for the new plants and mines in the Southwest as far back as 1953. Pollution has been around since then, as have emphysema and Black Lung. Utility experts were quick enough to commission studies on power needs

Nina Lansa, village chief,
Hopi

and profit and negotiate land leases with the Department of the Interior and the Indian tribes. Yet they ask us to believe that they had no time to consider pollution and plan for abatement equipment. One can only conclude that indeed they had no inclination to fight pollution because they were too eager to prepare for profit.

Clean air, open tracts of wilderness, pure water, native cultures—to industry these are esthetic, not economic, values. In a study like that made by the Westinghouse Corpora- tion for the Four Corners Regional Development Commission, therefore, they are given only several sentences in a 300-page opus. Electric can openers, fourteen-story casino signs, electric heating—these, according to the utilities, are essential to our civilization. And so, in their boundless dedication, the utilities and other related industries are doing all they can to give us the power to satisfy their needs. They will continue to do that until we, as a people, begin to assert our own.

Apache

EPILOGUE

As this book goes to press, Hopi warnings of the consequences of the destruction of the earth appear more and more real and more and more terrifying. Texas Eastern Transmission Corporation and Pacific Lighting Corporation have asked the Federal Power Commission to allow them to build a $4.6 million coal gasification plant near Farmington, New Mexico, which will use 9.6 million tons of coal from the Navajo mine and bring the Utah International Mining Company an additional $875 million over 25 years. If the application is granted, the plant will begin to operate in 1976. The Nixon administration has furthermore come out in favor of increasing coal development, by suggesting that oil and natural gas shortages can be avoided if more coal is used to fuel electrical generating plants. The administration refuses to advocate decreasing wasteful uses of power to offset predicted shortages.

And in spite of the outcry over the destruction of the Southwest, the utilities, coal companies, and the administration have decided to take progress elsewhere. The new scenario calls for the destruction of yet another unspoiled area in the United States—the tri-state area of Montana, Wyoming and North Dakota, where 42 mine-mouthed coal-fired generating plants are being planned to provide 53,000 megawatts of power for urban regions.

The Northern Cheyenne and Crow Indian Tribes are the new sacrificial victims, while many of the companies involved in the development are familiar, among them Peabody Coal Company. The various companies have threatened the Indians with condemnation of their surface land rights. And the promise of an influx of the 10,000 to 30,000 whites needed to run the plants could also mean de facto termination to the Northern Cheyenne, whose tribe numbers only 2,600. The plants will also affect thousands of ranchers in the region, who face the prospect of condemnation of surface rights as well as water shortages that will severely damage both ranching and agriculture. For this region, like the Southwest, is known for its water scarcity problems. The utilities plan to add to these problems by annually claiming 2.6 million acre-feet of water from the Tongue, Powder and Yellowstone Rivers, all major tributaries of the Missouri. The industry further estimates that an additional 300,000 to 500,000 people will be attracted to the area because of the development, again posing the problem of a megapolis supplied with unending amounts of electricity, and no water.

The environmental and social consequences of these plants are even more devastating than those we have outlined in the previous chapters, simply because the project is larger.

There are groups active in the area to fight this new attack on our air, land and water. And members of the Northern Cheyenne are challenging the leasing decision of a tribal council that has acted again in favor of industry and to the detriment of the tribe. But these groups, like those in the Southwest, must be supported by all Americans.

First it was the Southwest, now Montana, Wyoming and North Dakota —and next?

Suzanne Gordon

Jan. 16, 1973

ACTIVE ORGANIZATIONS

These organizations have been active in the struggle to keep the air, water and land of the Southwest pure and livable:

Black Mesa Defense Fund
770 Old Pecos Trail
Santa Fe, New Mexico 87501

Central Clearing House
338 East DeVargas
Santa Fe, New Mexico 87501

Sierra Club—all branches

Committee To Save Black Mesa
Box 569
Chinle, Arizona 86503

Native American Rights Fund
1506 Broadway
Boulder, Colorado 80302

Environmental Defense Fund
1712 N St. N.W.
Washington, D.C. 20036

National Wildlife Federation
1412 16th Street N.W.
Washington, D.C. 20036

Committee for Traditional
    Indian Land and Life
P.O. Box 74151
Los Angeles, California 90004

Friends of the Earth
529 Commercial Street
San Francisco, California 94111

DNA Legal Services
    (Navajo Legal Services)
Chinle, Arizona 86503

New Mexico Citizens for Clean Air
and Water
P.O. Box 4524
Albuquerque, New Mexico 87106

Albuquerque Environmental Center
1006 Tijeras N.W.
Albuquerque, New Mexico 87101

Students for Environmental Action
Ecology Information Center
Student Union Building
University of New Mexico
Albuquerque, New Mexico 87106

Page Citizens for Best Environment
Page, Arizona 86040

National Health and Environmental
    Law Program
2477 Law Building
405 Hilgard Avenue
Los Angeles, California 90024

Committee of Concern for the
    Traditional Indian
P.O. Box 5167
San Francisco, California 94101

RECOMMENDED READING

These books are highly readable, comprehensive investigations of various environmental issues and studies of the Indian tribes involved in the Black Mesa crisis.

Book of the Hopi, by Frank Waters. Ballantine Books.

Bury My Heart at Wounded Knee, by Dee Brown. Holt, Rinehart and Winston.

The Closing Circle: Nature, Man and Technology, by Barry Commoner. Alfred A. Knopf.

Custer Died for Your Sins: An Indian Manifesto, by Vine De Loria Jr. Avon.

Energy: A Crisis in Power, by John Holdren and Philip Herrera. A Sierra Club Battlebook.

The Fourth World of the Hopi, by Harold Courlander. Crown Publishers.

Mercury, by Katherine and Peter Montague. A Sierra Club Battlebook.

The Navajos: The Past and Present of a Great People, by John Upton Terrell. Perennial Library, Harper and Row.

The New Indians, by Stan Steiner. Dell Publishing Company.

Poisoned Power: the Case Against Nuclear Power Plants, by John W. Goffman and Arthur R. Tamplin. Rodale Press.

Stripping: The Surface Mining of America, by John F. Stacks. A Sierra Club Battlebook.

Timetable for Disaster, by Don Widener. Nash Publishing.

Vanishing Air: Nader Study Group Report on Air Pollution, by John C. Esposito. Grossman Publishers.

BIBLIOGRAPHY

Arizona Public Service Company, *1971 Annual Report*. Phoenix.

Birke, Gunnar, et al., "Studies on Humans Exposed to Methyl Mercury Through Fish Consumption," *Archives of Environmental Health*. Vol. 25, August, 1972.

Black Mesa Defense Fund, *Myths and Techno-Fantasies*. Santa Fe, New Mexico, 1972.

Brown, Dee, *Bury My Heart at Wounded Knee*. New York, Holt, Rinehart and Winston, 1970.

Budnick, Dan, "Black Mesa: Progress Report on an Ecological Rape." *Art in America*, Vol. 60, No. 4 (July-August 1972), pp. 96–105.

Bulletin of Atomic Scientists, "The Energy Crisis," parts one and two, Vol. XXVII, Nos. 7 and 8, 1971.

Chambers, Reid, *The Black Mesa Case Study*. Los Angeles, University of California Law School, 1971.

Clear Creek, magazine, *Black Mesa: Cultures in Collision*, Vol. 1, No. 13, 1972.

Clemmer, Richard O., *Economic Development vs. Aboriginal Land Use: An Attempt to Predict Culture Change on an Indian Reservation in Arizona*. Department of Anthropology, University of Illinois, 1970.

Council on Economic Priorities, *The Price of Power: Electric Utilities and the Environment*. Council on Economic Priorities, New York, 1972.

Committee for Traditional Indian Land and Life, *The Black Mesa Crisis*. Los Angeles, 1970.

Commoner, Barry, *The Closing Circle: Nature, Man and Technology*. Alfred A. Knopf, New York, 1971.

Courlander, Harold, *The Fourth World of the Hopi*. New York, Crown Publishers Inc., 1971.

De Loria, Vine Jr., *Custer Died for Your Sins: An Indian Manifesto*. New York, Avon, 1969.

Eastlake, William, "Black Mesa," *Earth Magazine*, Vol. 2, No. 2, 1971.

Esposito, John C., *Vanishing Air: Nader Study Group Report on Air Pollution*. New York, Grossman, 1970.

Fabricant, Neil, and Hallman, Robert M., *Toward a Rational Power Policy: Energy, Politics and Pollution*. New York, George Braziller, 1971.

Friends of the Earth, Coalition Against Strip Mining, *Stripping the Land of Coal: Only a Beginning*. San Francisco.

Fujimoto, Isao, *Navajos Not Satisfied*. An independent study.

Goffman, John W., and Tamplin, Arthur R., *Poisoned Power: The Case Against Nuclear Power Plants*. Emmaus, Pennsylvania, Rodale Press, 1971.

Goldsmith, M., *Geothermal Resources in California*. Pasadena, Environmental Quality Laboratory, California Institute of Technology, Report No. 5, 1971

Gregg, Kevin R., "White Man's Burden, Red Man's Land," *Earth Times*, Vol. 1, No. 3, pp. 20–28, 1970.

Grossman, Shelly and Mary, "Black Coal, Red Power," produced by WNET 13 New York, executive producer David Prowitt, created by Shelly and Mary Grossman, aired May, 1972.

Haley, Mary Jane, "Kilowatt Warlords of America," *Clear Creek*, Vol. 1, No. 7, pp. 8–11.

Holdren, John, and Herrera, Philip, *Energy: A Crisis in Power*. San Francisco and New York, Sierra Club, 1971.

Hull, Andrew P., *Some Comparisons of the Environmental Risks from Nuclear and Fossil Fueled Power Plants*. Upton, New York, Brookhaven National Laboratory.

Josephy, Alvin M., Jr., "Murder of the Southwest," *Audubon Magazine*, July, 1971 (Reprint).

Katchongva, Dan, *The Planting Stick: Hopi Teachings and Prophecies from the Beginning of Life to the Day of Purification*, as told by Dan Katchongva, Sun Clan. Interpreted by Danaqyumptewa and edited by Thomas V. Tarbet, Jr.

List, E.J., *Energy and the Environment in Southern California*. Pasadena, California, California Institute of Technology, 1971, reprinted from *Engineering and Science Magazine*, November 1971.

List, E.J., *Energy Use in California: Implications for the Environment*. Pasadena, Environmental Quality Laboratory, California Institute of Technology, Report No. 3, 1971.

Los Angeles County Air Pollution Control District, *Rules and Regulations*. 1971.

Los Angeles Department of Water and Power, *Seventh Annual Report, 1970–1971*.

Martin, J.E., et al., *Radioactivity from Fossil Fuel and Nuclear Power Plants*. U.S. Department of Health, Education and Welfare, Public Health Service, Environmental Health Service, Bureau of Radiological Health, Division of Environmental Radiation, 1970.

Montague, Katherine and Peter, *Mercury*. San Francisco and New York, Sierra Club Batlebook, 1971.

Newsweek, "The Big Clean-up," Vol. LXXIX, No. 24 (June 12, 1972), pp. 36–55.

Peabody Coal Company, *Mining Coal on Black Mesa*. St. Louis, 1971.

Rappaport, Roger, "Oops! The Story of Nuclear Power Plants," *Ramparts*, Vol. 10, No. 9 (March, 1972), pp. 49–57.

Regester, Richard, "Rage, Rage, Against the Dying of the Light," *West Magazine*, The Los Angeles *Times*, June 13, 1971, pp. 9–14.

Reilly, William P., *People, Progress and Power*. Arizona Public Service Company.

Salt River Project, *1970 Annual Report*. Phoenix, Arizona, Salt River Project.

Salt River Project, *1971 Annual Report*. Phoenix, Arizona, Salt River Project.

San Diego Gas and Electric Company, *1971 Annual Report*.

Scientific American, *Energy and Power*. San Francisco, W.H. Freeman and Company, 1971.

Southern California Edison Company, *1971 Annual Report*.

Stacks, John F., *Stripping: The Surface Mining of America*. San Francisco, Sierra Club, 1972.

Steiner, Stan, *The New Indians*. New York, Dell, 1968.

Terrell, John Upton, *The Navajos: the Past and Present of a Great People*. New York, Harper and Row, 1970.

U.S. Government, Bureau of National Affairs, *Air Standards and Criteria*. 1971.

U.S. Government, Bureau of National Affairs, *Energy Policy: President Nixon's Message to*

Congress and White House Fact Sheet, 1971.

U.S. Government, Committee on Interior and Insular Affairs, *Hearings on the Problems of Electrical Power Production in the Southwest.* U.S. Government Printing Office, Vols. 1–5, 1971.

U.S. Government, Committee on Interior and Insular Affairs, *Report on Problems of Electrical Power Production in the Southwest.* U.S. Government Printing Office, 1972.

U.S. Government, Department of Health, Education and Welfare, *Estimates of Air Pollution from the Four Corners Power Plant, New Mexico.* Public Health Service, 1970.

U.S. Government, Department of the Interior, *Draft Environmental Statement Navajo Project.* September, 1971.

U.S. Government, Department of the Interior, *Southwest Energy Study: An Evaluation of Electric Power Generation in the Southwest.* Draft summary and Vols. 1–12, 1972.

Waters, Frank, *Book of the Hopi.* New York, Ballantine, 1963.

Waters, Frank. *Masked Gods: Navajo and Pueblo Ceremonialism.* New York, Ballantine, 1950.

Westinghouse Corporation, *Four Corners Regional Development Study Program: A Study of Development Guidelines including the Analysis of Economic Potential and the Concept of a New Town for the Four Corners Region.* June, 1969.

Widener, Don, *Timetable for Disaster.* Los Angeles, Nash Publishing, 1970.